T0285656

TAMPA SPRING
TRAINING
TALES

TAMPA SPRING
TRAINING
TALES

MAJOR LEAGUE
MEMORIES

RICK VAUGHN

THE
History
PRESS

Published by The History Press
Charleston, SC
www.historypress.com

Front cover, top left: Courtesy of the Rhodes/Klumpe Reds Hall of Fame Collection; *top right*: Courtesy of Tampa Baseball Museum; *center left*: Courtesy of the Rhodes/Klumpe Reds Hall of Fame Collection; *bottom*: Courtesy of Savannah Bananas.
Back cover, top: Cardcow.com public domain; *inset*: Courtesy of the Tampa Baseball Museum.

First published 2024

Manufactured in the United States

ISBN 9781467156363

Library of Congress Control Number: 2023948356

CONTENTS

PREFACE

I saw only one game at Al Lopez Field. It was in March 1985, my first spring in baseball. I was the assistant public relations director of the Baltimore Orioles, and we had flown north from Miami to play the Cincinnati Reds in Tampa and the Philadelphia Phillies at Jack Russell Stadium in Clearwater on successive days. This was my first road trip. I was on the same chartered plane and the same buses with Baltimore legends Cal Ripken and Eddie Murray and the 1975 American League Rookie of the Year and MVP Fred Lynn. It was the beginning of a thirty-year dream. I made sure all my friends knew; especially the ones back home still shoveling snow from their driveways. But on that memorable trip, I had something else on my mind, something more pressing.

The morning before our game with the Reds, I was to take a quick cab ride (what we did before Uber) from our hotel on the Courtney Campbell Causeway to the Tampa Airport to pick up the first shipment of 1985 Oriole media guides. But this was no ordinary airport run. This was my first test. In some major league cities, the production of media guides may have been just a box to check off, but not in Baltimore. Their arrival might as well have been delivered by a Brink's convoy. My boss, Bob Brown, was the William Shakespeare of major league PR directors. This was his opus. Every word had to have a purpose. It was must-reading for beat writers around the major leagues.

Like everything else we did under Bob, this treasured treatise was thorough, exact and meticulously researched while containing more information than the Manhattan phone book. It was the result of our winter-long project aimed only at pleasing Bob. And that was not easy. There was a reason he was considered the best PR man in baseball and the second winner of the Robert O. Fishel Award, named after the former Yankees and league PR legend and given annually to a team director for public relations excellence. The first winner was Robert O. Fishel himself.

It was a shipment of twelve books—the rest would be sent to Bob at our spring headquarters at Miami Stadium. A veteran of many Grapefruit League road trips, Bob sent the rookie on this one with instructions to get the guides to the media as fast as humanly possible.

The paperback guide was 192 pages long, nine by four and a half inches in size and featured Jim Palmer, Al Bumbry and Ken Singleton on the cover, all beloved Orioles whose careers with the team had ended the season before. To me, the box that Bucky Bray from Baltimore's French-Bray Printing had put on the plane that morning from Baltimore might as well have contained the Pentagon Papers.

After a restless night dreaming about nothing but typos and my boss reacting to said typos, I fidgeted during the ride to the airport. Back in the cab with the box of guides in hand, I tore it open and spent the ten-minute ride to Al Lopez Field looking for mistakes, mistakes I would have missed as the proofreader of the final "blue line."

There would be a few teeny-weeny typos. It was inevitable. Every guide has them. I didn't see any during my quick perusal. Happily, I noted "Baltimore" and "Orioles" were spelled correctly on the cover. Eventually, I began breathing normally for the first time since we had left Miami. On arrival, I went straight to the press box and began proudly distributing the contents of the box to the writers from the *Baltimore Morning, Baltimore Evening Sun, Baltimore News-American, Washington Post* and a national writer or two.

By the time I was finished, the box contained two books. Just as the game started, a curious looking man with thinning black hair and horn-rimmed glasses approached me to ask if the Orioles media guides had arrived. He identified himself as Jim, but I didn't catch the last name. I was preoccupied, digging around in my travel bag in search of the Orioles scorebook.

I had no idea who he was, but there was no way anyone short of team president Larry Lucchino was prying these away. What if Peter Gammons or Jayson Stark were suddenly to appear and I had none to offer? The stranger seemed pretty upset when I held my ground, but he left without causing a scene.

Minutes later, Richard Justice, esteemed beat writer for the *Morning Sun*, sauntered over with a prescient look and asked me if I knew who that unhappy man was and what was it that I had I done to displease him. "Jim something," I replied as I turned my attention to my found scorebook. "I don't know him."

"Well, Bubba, maybe you should get to know him," responded Richard, who, over the next forty years, would torment me like only a great friend can. It was about to begin. "His name is Jim Russo, and he's only the guy who brought the Orioles Frank Robinson, Jim Palmer, Boog Powell and Mike Cuellar, that's all."

"No!" I shouted too loud for press box decorum.

"Yes!" he answered. "He's what they call a super scout."

Fortunately, I didn't have to look at Richard's grinning mug for long. I had already grabbed the two remaining books and was off looking for Al Lopez Field's scout seats, thinking how many bestsellers Bob Brown was going to throw at me when he found out I snubbed the chief architect of the Orioles' three World Series Championship teams. When I found Jim and handed him one of the precious publications, he actually smiled and said with what I'm sure was great delight, "I'll take two." He got two. The last two.

That auspicious introduction aside, Jim Russo was one of the people who made the "Oriole Way" the most desirable method of conducting the business of baseball in the 1960s, '70s and '80s. It was hard work but never without dignity, grace, discipline and respect for and loyalty to each other and our stakeholders. It was our unquestioned desire to uphold the Orioles' standing within the game as well as the Baltimore community that propelled us through fourteen-hour days from February to October. So much of that time was spent working together in our tiny offices at Memorial Stadium or in temporary spring training work spaces only slightly larger than an on-deck circle. It mattered.

This book is dedicated to Jim and all the others who taught me the Oriole Way. I wanted only to not disappoint them. They were Bob Brown, Phil Itzoe, Frank Robinson, Hank Peters, Jim Palmer, Cal Ripken Sr., Cal Ripken Jr., Brooks Robinson, Chuck Thompson, Larry Lucchino, Tom Giordano, Maeve Berkeridge, Helen Conklin, Charles Steinberg, Julie Wagner, Ken Nigro, Joe Hamper, Earl Weaver, Ann Lange, Mike Flanagan, Elrod Hendricks, Rex Barney, Johnny Oates, Ernie Tyler and his sons, Jon Miller, Janet Marie Smith, Roy Sommerhof, Audrey Brown, Vernon Joyner, Fred Trautman, David Shauck, Ralph Salvon and Richie Bancells. Also included were Helen and Hazel, who prepared our dinners each night in the press dining room with so much care; two leaders I never met in Frank Cashen and Harry Dalton; and Phyllis Merhige, who often counseled me like a big sister from the league offices in New York.

That group was so dedicated to doing the right thing. They all taught me so much. They cared, and the players and citizenry of Baltimore cared right back. It wasn't by accident. Without them, I would have had no career in the game I have loved my whole life. Thank you for guiding me through the best times of my three-decades-long career in baseball and for never letting me forget what a privilege it was to "work" in Major League Baseball. I was so honored to be an Oriole, to be an adopted Baltimorean. We were truly one and the same.

INTRODUCTION

At the 1959 dedication of the iconic Busch Gardens, founder August Busch Jr. noted that it was spring visits with his St. Louis Cardinals baseball team that acquainted him with Tampa Bay and led to his decision to erect what has long been Tampa's biggest tourist attraction.

Just as it did in 1959, baseball assumed varying roles in the development of more than twenty cities across Florida in the twentieth century—in Tampa's case, even earlier. "Many accounts suggest that returning prisoners [of the Civil War] brought it from the North, but regardless you had organized baseball being played by the 1870s and certainly by the 1880s," theorized author and historian Gary Mormino. "And clearly the formation of Ybor provided a spark."

Tampa's Ybor City was the "cigar capital of the world" at the time and home to those early teams, whose rosters were filled with hardworking cigar factory workers from Cuba, Spain and Italy, all struggling to find their way in a new world. It was baseball that helped bring them together. "I've never heard people say specifically that baseball was the uniting force in Ybor City, but it had to be a uniting force. It was the universal language," said Elizabeth McCoy, curator of the Tampa Baseball Museum.

"In the first years of the twentieth century, no other southern city was as synonymous with baseball as Tampa," wrote University of South Florida professor Paul Dunder. "Street corners, recreational parks, and local stadiums all became sites of baseball. Mutual-aid societies [Centro-Espanol, L'Union Italiana, El Circulo Cubano, El Porvenir], cigar factories, and city neighborhoods all established teams and leagues. Baseball was part of the immigrant and working-class experience in the city. Its growth in popularity paralleled the city's industrial development. As the cigar factories grew, so did the importance of baseball in the city."

"While baseball had been popular only among Ybor City's Cubans in the late 1880's," wrote historian and author Wes Singletary, "by the 1920's it had community-wide acceptance."

Hall of Fame manager Tony LaRussa, a Tampa native whose parents met when they were both working at the Perfecto-Garcia cigar factory in Ybor, told the *St. Petersburg Times* in 2014 that baseball was "dominant to the point of being a religion—especially with my Italian and Spanish background."

And though "Cigar City" more accurately describes Tampa's past rather than the present, with nearly all the cigar factories closed, many of today's Tampeños have relatives who worked in the factories. Then there's four-time World Series Champion Tino Martinez, who won a state championship at Tampa Catholic High School as a freshman first baseman and was later a first-round draft choice out of the University of Tampa. He worked at a cigar factory from the time he was twelve through his high school years with his brothers Rene Jr. and Tony.

The Martinez family lived on Kathleen Street in West Tampa, one block from the Villazon Cigar factory in a house Tino's mother still lives in today. Tino's father, Rene, was the general manager at the factory. During the summer months and at Christmas breaks from school, Rene "recruited" his three sons to help unload the heavy bales of tobacco leaves from Honduras off the incoming semi-trucks. "It wasn't just once in a while, we would unload all day long," Martinez told me. "It was just hard labor, heavy labor. But it was great, it was a great learning experience. If we had a game that day, we would leave work around noon and walk home and get lunch and get ready for the game." It was baseball and work at the cigar factory all summer long for Tino and his brothers, as they carried on a tradition that began when his grandparents came to Florida decades before.

According to the *Tampa Bay Times*, there were "more than 200 factories at the peak of Tampa's cigar industry. Today, two dozen remain. Only one still produces cigars, and around half are protected as local historic landmarks."

Cigar factory workers in Ybor City. *Courtesy of Tampa-Hillsborough County Public Library.*

While the cigar industry in Tampa is largely unlit today, the baseball fire still burns. Beginning with the city's baseball patriarch, Hall of Fame catcher-manager Al Lopez, who debuted with the Brooklyn Robins in 1928, Tampa has produced ninety major leaguers, according to the Tampa Baseball Museum. "What the Chesapeake Bay is to crabs, Tampa is to baseball: a rich breeding ground, known for both quantity and quality," wrote George Will in his book *Men at Work.*

Longtime *Tampa Tribune* sportswriter Joey Johnston covered local high school matchups that featured the likes of future major league all-stars Dwight Gooden pitching against Fred McGriff and Jose Fernandez facing Pete Alonzo. "What was that like?" he was asked recently. "Just another Tuesday in Tampa," he replied.

Like cigars, Cuban sandwiches and annual pirate invasions, baseball *is* Tampa. That is especially true in the spring, when, for most of the last 111 years, the city and its people have excelled as hosts of Major League Baseball. No one has done it longer. Since 1913, that historic run has included affiliations with the Cubs, Red Sox, Senators, Tigers, Reds, White Sox and Yankees covering three ballparks: Plant Field, Al Lopez Field and George M. Steinbrenner Field née Legends Field, palatial spring residence of the Yankees since 1996. The only thing Tampa lacked—as evidenced by multiple springs of mediocre home attendance—was summed up by *Tribune* sportswriter Ralph Warner in 1954: "Tampa hasn't been a tourist city in the past, isn't one now and won't be in the indefinite future."

But it was in Tampa where the first Grapefruit League no-hitter was thrown; where Babe Ruth hit his longest home run (and was reportedly shot in the leg by a jealous ex-girlfriend from Ybor City); and where Ted Williams batted nearly .400 as a visitor and spat at the fans, five years before he did so in a notorious episode at Fenway Park.

It was where Jackie Robinson went 4-for-4 and stole home as part of a triple steal; where a 1925 game between defending league champions, the Senators and Giants, featured twelve players bound for Cooperstown; where both the Big Red Machine and the Core Four first gathered; where Jeter became shortstop and Charley Hustle was born; where Tom Seaver, the only pitcher in the last ninety years with 4,000 career innings and a sub-3.00 ERA, once gave up 10 runs in a game; where Walter Johnson broke his ankle and George Brett tore knee ligaments; where a nineteen-year-old catcher named Johnny Bench caught three Mets trying to steal in one afternoon while Yogi Berra watched the next big thing from the opposing dugout; where a pitcher with exactly one career win—Washington's Ralph Lumenti—bested Hall of

Famer Early Wynn, who won exactly 300; where Sparky Anderson earned the first of 120 wins in his first season as a major league manager; and where, in the same spring, Roberto Clemente and Frank Robinson each hit their first home run in a major league uniform. Finally, it could only be in Tampa where the city's baseball patriarch, Al Lopez, was ejected from a game in a ballpark bearing his name.

From the outset, the Tampa Bay Hotel, followed by the Floridan and Tampa Terrace, learned how to handle the needs of major league players. So efficient was the Floridan that for two days in March 1955, the hotel accommodated three teams at the same time, wrote *The Sporting News*.

The city launched the annual Governor's Baseball Dinner in 1947 and played gracious host to twenty of the first twenty-two spring shindigs. For years, National League executives held their annual spring dinner at Tampa's Columbia Restaurant, and it was there on March 12, 1952, that the Yankees announced their all-time team in celebration of the franchise's fiftieth anniversary.

Tampa's central location allowed its teams to return in time for dinner after most road games. For the same reason, scouts often used Tampa as their hub. And for many years, according to *The Sporting News*, the Reds' welcoming press room on the fourth floor at the Floridan was "the watering hole for every itinerant columnist who made the annual trek [to spring training]."

Tampa even had what sportswriters dubbed "the Toots Shor's of Tampa," the very fine Spanish Park Restaurant located at Thirty-Sixth Street and East Broadway in Ybor City. Owner Joe Valdes saw to it that his was one of the few restaurants that advertised in *The Sporting News*, touting full-course,

The Spanish Park Restaurant was a favorite of baseball executives, writers and players. *Courtesy of LaGaceta.*

Plant Field was home to spring training baseball games from 1913 to 1954. In this photo, preparation for the Florida State Fair has begun on the field's main diamond in front of the grandstand. *Courtesy of Tampa-Hillsborough County Public Library*.

authentic Spanish meals for $1.50 in the 1950s. In his "What Is Spring Training?" column, Joe Falls of the *Detroit Free Press* began with the "black bean soup at the Spanish Park Restaurant."

In 1932, Frank Grayson, sports editor of the *Cincinnati Times-Star*, wrote simply, "Tampa possesses a certain continental charm that is not found elsewhere in this opulent state." His colleague Tom Swope from the *Cincinnati Post* took it a step further. "Having been in Tampa with the Cincinnati Reds through 17 different training seasons, I have come to regard that city as a sort of second home. So do many of Cincinnati's players and club officials."

Some took up temporary residences removed from the Tampa style of living at nearby MacDill Air Force Base and found the same hospitality, with one telling *The Sporting News* that the accommodations were "the nicest they have ever seen for rent in any spring training camp."

Except for the first week of just about every spring, when the diamond at Plant Field was rebounding from the pounding it took from Florida State Fair revelers, the playing surface was one of the finest. What's more, it was on the same grounds as the team's Tampa Bay Hotel headquarters. When the White Sox began workouts at Al Lopez Field in 1954, General Manager Frank Lane, always open to discuss a trade, remarked that he wouldn't swap the practice grounds in Tampa for the Comiskey Park infield.

While many of Tampa's businesses complied with the discriminating state and local Jim Crow laws that plagued the South until the Civil Rights Act of 1964, Plant Field might have been one of the few places to occasionally relax those racist restrictions. Sportswriter Warren Brown of the *Chicago American* was one of more than seven thousand attendees who jammed the ballpark for a game between the Jackie Robinson–led Dodgers and the host White Sox in 1954. "A conference between Sox General Manager Frank Lane and his aids resulted in a decision to open up more rows of grandstand seats for the Negro patrons. Anyone who cared to take note must have discovered that no one, Negro or white, gave any thought to segregation or desegregation. Negroes and whites whooped it up alike as the fortunes of the game and players changed. There wasn't the slightest trace of disorder. It struck me at the time without the soapbox orator or his modern-day counterpart, this matter would adjust itself in all things Southern just as it was proven it could do in a ballpark in Tampa."

For fifty-four years, the city and the Reds built a partnership based on loyalty and trust that endured eight different Reds ownership groups and thirteen mayors. There were challenges. Between 1925 and 1961, Tampa trained just one World Champion. Nearby St. Petersburg, with the Yankees teams of Ruth, Gehrig, Mantle and DiMaggio and the Cardinals of Musial, Gibson, Hornsby and Dean thrilling tourists, hosted nineteen. It was a *big* shadow.

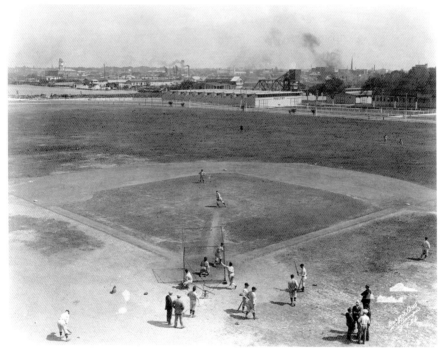

The defending World Champion Washington Senators working out on the practice diamond at Plant Field in 1925. *Courtesy of Tampa-Hillsborough County Public Library System.*

Nonetheless, Tampa was selected over St. Petersburg and Miami for the one-time spring training All-Star Game in 1940, a heralded event that produced Florida's largest baseball crowd at the time. Wrote Swope, "Although St. Petersburg, with two teams training there annually, long has been regarded as the spring training capital of Florida's west coast, Tampa has been in the major league spring training picture longer and just as consistently as the 'Sunshine City.'"

Tampa, specifically Plant Systems of Steamboats and Railroads, made a bid to lure the Reds from their Columbus, Georgia spring training home in 1899, according to the *Cincinnati Enquirer*. The Reds wanted all of their transportation and hotel costs covered. On February 18, the *Enquirer* wrote that the negotiations had ended and that Reds' business manager had informed the owners of the grounds at Columbus to "put up the stoves in the dressing room and to arrange for a plentiful supply of warm water." It wasn't until thirty-two years later that the Reds and Tampa struck a deal.

Although no major league team had ventured south of St. Augustine for spring training, it was only a matter of time before the major leagues took notice of the advantages that Tampa offered, if nothing else as a desirable location to visit while either coming or going from their offseason barnstorming trips to Cuba.

In 1900, the National League's Brooklyn Superbas and New York Giants were scheduled to play games in Jacksonville and Tampa on their way to Cuba, but delays forced them to skip Tampa.

It wasn't until October 1908 that a major league team finally made an appearance in the Cigar City. On their way to Cuba, the Reds, with second baseman and future Hall of Fame manager Miller Huggins, visited for a pair of games against the semipro Tampa Perfectos. The Reds prevailed, 11–3 and 11–0, as the locals committed 13 errors. The series was shortened by one game when it was discovered that the team's equipment was left at the railway station in Chattanooga. Manager Dave Bancroft, a future Hall of Famer, and his wife, Edna, toured a cigar factory, and players went fishing on the unexpected off day.

Earlier that month, Tampeños were so excited about the Cubs-Tigers World Series that the city became one of the first in the South to install a local telegraph connection carrying a pitch-by-pitch account of the games. For admission prices of fifteen or twenty-five cents, fans at Tampa's new Orpheum Theatre could follow the game called by an "expert announcer," according to the *Tampa Tribune*. A written account of the action was kept on a blackboard set up in the front of the theater.

A huge throng gathered at the telegraphic scoreboard on the exterior of the *Tampa Tribune* building to follow the progress of the Athletics' win over the Giants in Game Seven of the 1913 World Series. Tampa Tribune *photo*.

The following year, the Detroit Tigers, minus future Hall of Famers Ty Cobb and Sam Crawford, handed the Perfectos a 9–1 setback on their way south. Attendance for that October 28 game was four hundred, producing $168.73 in total receipts, according to the *Tampa Tribune*. Of that, $101.25 went to the American League champions.

Al Lopez Field. *Tampa Bay History Center photo.*

Not a lot of money changed hands, but the fire was lit under Tampa mayor Donald B. McKay, who wanted a team for a variety of reasons. Baseball again was about to bring positive change. Wrote Dunder, "The city was still reeling from the 1910–11 [cigar industry] labor strike that had financially crippled the city and furthered the ethnic and class divide. To remedy this, spring training baseball was seen as something that could both financially uplift the city while also promoting some sort of reconciliation."

As such, baseball-crazy Tampa, with its cigar and phosphorous industries and a population nearly seven times that of its conservative neighbor across the bay, St. Petersburg, became just the third Florida city to host a major league spring training camp, joining Jacksonville and St. Augustine, when the Chicago Cubs arrived in 1913. (The Cleveland Indians and Pensacola city officials announced a spring training agreement nine days after the Cubs agreed to come to Tampa.) Among other things, the Chicago club's decision was influenced by the trappings of the Tampa Bay Hotel.

And just as it was the fervor for amateur and semipro baseball that helped define Tampa and inspired city leaders to court the Grapefruit League, it was the influence of those major leaguers who followed that brought prosperity in different forms. One was the Annual Tony Saladino High

School Tournament, among the top prep tournaments in the country and a Tampa treasure. A Ybor City native, Tony Saladino Jr., fell in love with the game while watching his heroes every spring. He paid it forward by dedicating his life to the amateur game and forged relationships with many of the young stars. Now in its forty-third year, the tournament is named for his father, Tony Saladino Sr. Dwight Gooden was the tournament's first Most Valuable Player in 1981, and future major leaguer Dave Magadan signed his college scholarship papers to Alabama in Tony's living room. Tony knows them all: Gooden, Magadan, Carl Everett, Tino Martinez, Fred McGriff, Gary Sheffield, Wade Boggs and Floyd Youmans among them.

Team photo from the 1924 Florida State League Tampa Smokers at Plant Field. *Courtesy of Tampa-Hillsborough County Public Library System.*

Throughout it all, Tampa's most endearing team may have been none of those major league clubs. It was the Smokers, a team whose name was chosen to reflect the cigar industry, that in various years from 1919 to 1954 competed in the Florida State League (FSL), Southeastern League and Florida International League. Few professional teams, regardless of the sport, have made a grander entrance than the Smokers. After finishing last in their first season in the FSL, they followed that up by going 89-28 (.760), an improvement of 350 percentage points and still the best record in FSL history. Five years later, they signed Tampa's beloved son, sixteen-year-old Al Lopez, to his first pro contract.

1

THE PALACE OF A PRINCE

Eight years ago, a wilderness of brush and undergrowth met the eye where now stands a suburban city. The magnificent hotel built by H.B. Plant, mammoth in proportion, unrivaled in architectural design, second to none in the entire south, looms up with grounds so artistically designed affording drives, promenades, boat exercises, gymnastic sports, amid a great intermingling of orange, date, palmetto and every species of tropical shrubbery and fruit of every variety may be seen growing in these grounds as much at home as if seen in their native Isles. The wonder is how such a change has been wrought in so short a time.
—Tampa Morning Tribune, *October 13, 1893*

Henry Plant's magical Tampa Bay Hotel and its beautiful 150-acre grounds may have helped Tampa emerge from its tropical jungle beginnings. It may have given the city a sense of place. It was Tampa's first tourist destination, drawing four thousand well-heeled tourists in its first year. And it was the headquarters for the U.S. military during the Spanish-American War.

An 1897 promotional brochure advertised the recently opened luxury resort as "the palace of a prince." Without it, Tampa may not have begun its long run as a spring training host when it did. And yet, somehow, the infamous Bambi Motel in Gainesville, which rented rooms by the hour, had a longer run.

The Tampa Bay Hotel was known for its Byzantine minarets, cantilevered balconies, Gothic windows and keyhole arches, a style that in the end

Left: The Tampa Bay Hotel was spring training headquarters for the major league teams training in Tampa from 1913 to 1931. The teams played at Plant Field on the hotel grounds. *Courtesy of Tampa-Hillsborough County Public Library System.*

Right: The Tampa Bay Hotel veranda. *Courtesy of Tampa-Hillsborough County Public Library System.*

worked against Plant as another form of architecture emerged. "A Spanish renaissance classical, cleaner look was advancing. Plant ended up with a wonderful building that looked backward in the 19th century," said art historian Susan Braden in the museum's informational video.

But baseball people don't care about architecture. They care about superior comfort, convenience and consistency. The Cubs found all three at the luxurious resort when they became the first team to train in Tampa, in 1913. "Our players are used to the best of accommodations when traveling and they should have them in the spring also," said team owner Charles W. Murphy. "The hotel is a palace and the ballfield is right back of it."

The hotel had the state's first elevator. There were also telephones and indoor plumbing with private baths in every suite. And there was a ball field inside a racetrack on the hotel grounds. In the evening, players would often sit out on the lawn near a bandstand and listen to music.

The December 6, 1897 *Tampa Tribune* noted the start of construction on the hotel's racetrack. It would become the first large spectator-sport facility in the area. As the work continued, the *Tribune* noted the following October: "The 8 acres of ground that is surrounded by the track has been planted in Bermuda grass…and the enclosure will make a very pretty field, and an excellent place for baseball, golf, tennis, and athletic contests for which it will be utilized." Susan V. Carter, curator of the Henry B. Plant Museum, said, "We do know that Mr. Plant had a Plant System Baseball team in the 1890's and we think they practiced on the hotel grounds, at or near Plant Field." It

Plant Field construction in 1899, with the South Florida Fair Board of Governors posing in front. *Courtesy of Florida Photograph Collection.*

wasn't long before the hotel's racetrack was expanded from a quarter mile to a half mile to better accommodate sports like baseball and auto racing.

One of the early games played on the hotel grounds was the barnstorming Bloomer Girls versus the semipro Tampa Greys in March 1899.

In 1900, as part of the city's Fourth of July celebration, there was horse racing and baseball on the grounds. In their advance of the game, the *Tribune* wrote: "The game features two teams composed of prominent citizens. There is a lively spirit of rivalry between the two teams, and some records and perhaps limbs will be broken. The teams represent the east and west sides of Franklin Street and much money has been placed on the game. A particular bet is two to one that the score on each side will run over 100."

To accommodate the new City Baseball League in 1908, league directors received a lease from the city on the field on the hotel grounds. The lease had been bought by the city in 1905 following Plant's death six years earlier. Improvements were in order. The hope was that the establishment of a good athletic field might help in efforts to bring a big-league team to the city for spring training. Later that year, the Reds did indeed play there on their way to Cuba.

In addition to the ninety-four baseball Hall of Famers who trod on the grounds from 1913 until the Reds' final workout there in 1962, icons such as boxer John L. Sullivan, football star Red Grange, Olympian Jim Thorpe, showman Buffalo Bill Cody and Teddy Roosevelt spent time there.

The White Sox and Reds played at Plant until 1954 before both moved to Al Lopez Field for games the following year. Cincinnati continued to hold early spring workouts at Plant before the City of Tampa built a training complex adjacent to Al Lopez Field for the 1963 season.

Opposite: A large group of people file through the entrance to the Florida State Fair Grounds at Plant Field. The baseball diamond can be seen to the right. *Courtesy of Florida Photograph Collection.*

Left: Columbia Restaurant's parade float headed for the Florida State Fair Grounds at Plant Field in 1937. *Courtesy of Tampa-Hillsborough County Public Library.*

Minor league baseball, college and high school baseball and football, horse racing, car racing and much more took place on the grounds. The University of Tampa (UT) gridiron squad played its home games on Plant Field from 1933 to 1936. The first state fair was held there in 1904 and remained until 1975.

The grounds had been known as Tampa Bay Park, or the Fairgrounds, or City Park until September 16, 1913. On that date at a city council meeting, it was agreed that "the area surrounding the Tampa Bay Hotel will be known as Plant Park." As a result of that resolution, the baseball field became known as Plant Field.

In 1933, the city signed a lease with UT giving the university the right to use the building for one hundred years at the cost of one dollar a year. Today, a portion of the building and its grounds continues to serve the university, which took over Plant Field in the early 1970s and renamed it Peppin-Rood Stadium after university benefactors. While a portion of the old playing surface is still in use as part of newer venues, the last remaining piece of Plant Field's old grandstand was torn down in 2002.

2

A HAPPY NEW YEAR

Aside from the agreeable weather and first-class accommodations, the controversial owner of the Chicago Cubs, Charles W. Murphy, offered another reason for wanting to move his team from New Orleans to Tampa Bay for spring training in 1913. "Seasickness," said Murphy, apparently envisioning his team traveling south to Tampa over the Gulf of Mexico, "is the best thing in the world to start training on, as it rids the system of the winter's accumulation of luxuries and minor ills incident to a life of laziness." This quote came from the man who would decide the first baseball turf war between Tampa and St. Petersburg. Both cities were vying for the Cubs, who were looking to become the first major league team to train south of St. Augustine.

Although the Cubs won four National League pennants and two World Series during his eight years of ownership, Murphy was better known for his domineering than his championships. Wrote SABR's Lenny Jacobsen: "His behind-the-scenes machinations and bombastic comments in the press made him numerous enemies." He was "independence personified," wrote Jason Cannon in his book *Charlie Murphy: The Iconoclastic Showman behind the Chicago Cubs*.

His baseball career began in 1905, when he was hired by the New York Giants as the first public relations man a baseball club had ever employed. From his position on the inside, the thirty-seven-year-old Murphy soon learned that the Cubs were up for sale. It didn't take long for him to secure a loan from a friend and purchase 51 percent of the team.

Cubs owner Charles W.
Murphy. *Courtesy of Chicago
History Museum.*

Offenses aside, Murphy was also somewhat of a visionary, which likely contributed to the disdain he experienced from his fellow owners. Cannon wrote that in 1907, Murphy first brought about the idea of players wearing numbers of the backs of their jerseys, and according to the January 21, 1912 *Tampa Tribune*, he raised the idea of a winter instructional league for Florida. Uniform numbers were adopted in 1937, and the Florida Instructional League debuted in 1958.

There was one other incentive for Murphy to consider moving his team south: a group of Tampa businessmen led by Mayor Donald B. McKay was willing to pay the opportunistic Cubs owner. It didn't hurt that McKay was also the editor and publisher of the *Tribune*.

In its January 9, 1913 edition, *The Sporting News* wrote: "The good people of Tampa had raised $4,700 to defray the expenses of the Cubs while advertising the Florida resort. Score one more step in the commercialization of the nation's pastime. It was bound to come—this conversion of a baseball team's advertising value into cash and so far as known, the Cub boss was the first to put into concrete form. There may have been subsidies along the same line, in different form, in the training arrangements of major league clubs in previous years, but this is the first deal of its kind that we can recall."

Sam Crane of the *New York Evening Journal* piled on. "Charles Murphy, president of the Chicago club, has no sentiment for baseball, only for the money there may be in it for him. In fact, the 'Chubby One' is considered a joke all over the National League, and nowhere more so than in Chicago." Not so in Tampa and St. Petersburg, where their fierce competition for Murphy's Cubs continued until two months before the start of spring training. They may have believed that Murphy was merely ahead of his time.

On Christmas Eve, the *St. Petersburg Times*, perhaps influenced by the spirit of the season, proclaimed, "City Has Inside Track to Land Cubs." But the stylishly dressed, rotund Murphy was in Tampa on December 30, agreeing to a deal on New Year's Eve in the offices of Tampa's Board of Trade.

St. Petersburg tried, but Tampa, with a population of roughly forty thousand to St. Pete's six thousand, outmuscled the Sunshine City. The long-lasting baseball competition between the two cities was on.

Vicente Martinez Ybor, owner of one of the city's first cigar manufacturing companies, was among those who helped raise the funds for Tampa's bid. Also in that supportive group were Lykes Co., Tampa Electric and Rinaldi Printing, all in existence today. Calling the city's business leaders "live wires," Murphy stated, "I like Tampa and its businessmen because of their businesslike manner in which they take hold of a proposition." Unspoken, of course, was Tampa's willingness to give Murphy their money.

It may have also been the work of one businessman in particular that helped tip the scales in Tampa's favor. H.M. Stanford, manager of the Tampa Bay Hotel, drew Murphy's praise. "In the Tampa Bay Hotel you have the best and most beautiful American plan hotel that it has ever been my pleasure to be in," he told the *Tampa Morning Tribune* after signing the deal. He added, "I can't leave without complementing its aggressive manager."

On the before day the deal was announced, St. Petersburg city officials sent Murphy the following message via telegram: "We can't give you the Tampa Bay Hotel, we will give you St. Petersburg." It wasn't enough.

Stanford had come to the Tampa landmark in 1911 from the acclaimed Continental Hotel in Atlantic Beach. During his time there, it is possible that he may have been positively influenced by the presence of the Dodgers, who trained in nearby Jacksonville.

In 1912, Stanford sent letters to all sixteen major league teams inviting them to Tampa in the spring, and he was present when the Tampa City Council introduced a resolution to extend an invitation to Murphy in April. He was eventually named president of the Mid-Winter Baseball Association, the group overseeing the Cubs' presence in Tampa.

On returning home to Chicago, Murphy was beaming. The January 8 *Tampa Tribune* quoted him as boasting: "It's the best training spot in the world and it looks as if we'll be training there for several years to come. The players can sit in the dining room of the hotel right above the Hillsborough River and while they are eating their soup they can catch their fish from the windows. There's a clubhouse on the ballfield with shower baths and I didn't see any mosquitos. There's a fine grass diamond there now, but I'm going to send Charley Kuhn, our groundskeeper, to Tampa next week to fix it up in first class shape."

Kuhn arrived on January 9 and quickly realized that his boss may have exaggerated about the condition of the field within the hotel's oval racetrack. The *Tampa Tribune* described it as looking "really bad, but when Mayor McKay had assured him [Kuhn] that a gang of prisoners and anything else needed to put the grounds in proper shape was here for the asking, he became quite optimistic." (At the time, it was common for cities to "lease" inmates from state prisons or city jails for manual-labor projects.)

On January 29, sod from the far end of the racetrack oval was cut out and placed on the diamond. The prisoners assigned to the work project installed plumbing for showers and toilets and laid cement for the clubhouse floors and walls. They also brought in clay to fill low spots along the playing surface.

Rather than the boat ride that Murphy envisioned, the Cubs arrived in Tampa aboard Seaboard train number 99 just before dinner on February 17. Thirty-six members of the team's traveling party, weary from their two-and-a-half-day trip sans air-conditioning, were met by a large number of prominent citizens and members of the Mid-Winter Baseball Association, who were wearing badges that read, "Cubs take Tampa and the Rag," a reference to the National League pennant.

The party was then ushered to the Tampa Bay Hotel for a celebratory meal. On the team's arrival, it was soon discovered that Murphy had failed to reserve rooms for the Cubs' twelve-member media contingent. It was likely no accident. Three years before at baseball's winter meetings in New York, he was quoted in *The Sporting News* as saying, "Baseball can get along without the newspapers better than the newspapers can get along without baseball."

Hotel manager Stanford remedied the situation after some harsh words were directed at Murphy from the scribes, according to the *Tampa Tribune*. The sportswriters passed the time waiting for their rooms in the hotel's billiards room.

As the players took a day of preparation, work began on the installation of some five hundred bleacher seats on the first-base side, bringing the total capacity of Plant Field to three thousand.

It had to be a strange scene for the Cubs, who were without two-thirds of their Hall of Fame double play combination, Tinker to Evers to Chance. The trio had made history together for the ten previous seasons, even becoming the subject of a celebrated poem by Franklin Pierce Adams. Shortstop Joe Tinker had been traded to the Reds, and first baseman Frank Chance had been fired by Murphy as player-manager. Second baseman Johnny Evers was the lone survivor as Chance's replacement as player-manager, one of a quartet of managers the Cubs would employ during their four years of training in Tampa.

The players began their workouts on February 19, only to find that the fields were not in shape and the facilities insufficient. Wrote historian James Covington: "Due to heavy rains the ground was too soft and spongy, and the roller had done a poor job on the infield. In addition, the shower

Left: Cubs player-manager Johnny Evers was the only member of the famous Tinker to Evers to Chance double-play combination left when the Cubs arrived in Tampa in 1913. *Courtesy of Library of Congress.*

Right: The first two future Hall of Famers to grace Plant Field were Evers and catcher Roger Bresnahan (*pictured*). *Courtesy of Library of Congress.*

facilities were not finished, there was no hot water and the players had to walk back to the hotel and bathe in their rooms, which had hot water. Mayor D.B. McKay ordered emergency overtime work to get the grounds in shape. The infield was cleared and resodded with Bermuda grass in the center and clay from the race track on the base paths, better drains were dug and showers and lockers were constructed in the Woman's Building of the fairgrounds. While these changes were being made, the pitchers were able to work out, but the others played soccer and basketball and ran around the race track."

One day, at least part of their workout consisted of chasing a rabbit off the diamond in what surely was an early team-building exercise. In another of the spring's unusual scenes, the Cubs worked out on the last Saturday of February while motorcycle races took place on the surrounding oval, a promotion arranged by the Tampa Bay Hotel's intrepid Stanford.

With no major league opponents scheduled, it was proposed that the Cubs would open the spring with a series against an amateur team from Cuba, the Havana Athletics. As arrangements were being made to transport the Cuban team to Tampa, one issue had to be settled. The February 7 *Tampa*

Tribune reported on a meeting of the city's Mid-Winter Baseball Association: "The question of Negro was raised regarding the Cuban team and those present were assured that the entire team would be composed of pure white Cubans." This of course would explain why the Cubans were allowed to take lodging at the Tampa Bay Hotel. (Three days after the Athletics left Tampa to return to Cuba, Booker T. Washington, educator and civil rights activist and arguably the most influential Black man in America, spoke to a group at the hotel. He was not permitted to stay overnight.)

Wrote Covington: "The Athletics, 21 in number including 16 players, two officials and three newspapermen according to the *Chicago Tribune*, traveled aboard the Mascotte from Havana before landing at Port Tampa on February 20. They were greeted by Consul Rafael M. Ybor and members of the Cuban community and escorted to the Tampa Bay Hotel." Individual tickets priced at fifty and seventy-five cents went fast. According to Covington, the hardware firm of Knight and Wall donated the balls.

The first game scheduled for February 24 was postponed due to wet grounds, but both teams were able to work out, and the local hosts made time to take the "gentlemen of the press" on a tour of Tampa that included, according to the *Tampa Tribune*, "the inner workings of the cigar industry and many other novel sights."

Two days later, with the field finally in game shape, they tried again. Under sunny skies, the Cubs defeated the Athletics, 4–2, before a huge throng described as six thousand by the *Chicago Tribune*.

The story in the *South Bend (IN) Tribune* praised the atmosphere. "A stranger landing in Tampa would have thought it was a real world's championship from the enthusiasm displayed on every street corner and the tremendous crowd that thronged the lone entrance to get a chance to pay their coin for tickets. The game was worth the price, too. Instead of making mincemeat of the little foreigners, the Cubs had to play some real baseball in order to get the big end of the boxscore."

"It was by far the largest gathering to an athletic affair ever held in Tampa and the crowd was equaled only by that which crammed the same grounds to hear William Jennings Bryan speak four years before," wrote the *Tribune*. "The game was not up to big league form, but far exceeded the class of ball seen on local lots."

The *Tribune* added, "It was remarked by an unnamed citizen that the crowd furnished a striking instance of Tampa's growth. There are more automobiles in this park this afternoon than there were horse drawn vehicles in this city ten years ago."

It was also reported that an agreement was made with Special Officer Thomas, "one of the best crook nabbers in the business," to lead security at the park. He likely earned his pay on Opening Day. The large crowd, which was nearly one-half Cuban, posed another problem for city officials. Ticket takers at the field's three gates could not handle the demand, and it wasn't until the second inning that all were finally seated. To help the mood, the Tampa Municipal Band played for the fans.

According to Covington, "Some fans sneaked into the game through open fences. In addition to long automobile and ticket-selling lines, people found many mistakes in the printed program."

In the remaining two games, the Cubans were beaten, 12–4 and 17–1 before crowds of three thousand and two thousand, respectively. Cubs third baseman Arty Phelan hit the first home run, a high line drive that was misjudged by right fielder Dominguez, who then failed to run after the ball. "The sulky outfielder was removed from the game by his manager and Loma was sent in to replace him," wrote the *Chicago Tribune*. "The Cuban spectators hissed the crab as he left the field."

Attendance remained respectable for the games against the Athletics, partly because some cigar factories dismissed their workforce early, allowing employees to attend the games. But interest waned for the remaining seven games, six of which were intrasquad games and one against a local amateur squad. Admission for those games was reduced to twenty-five cents. Hopes of adding another series with the Cubans didn't materialize, because a number of Cuban players had to return to their jobs.

According to the *Tampa Tribune*, the winning team in those intrasquad games got a box of cigars, with the "ropes" to be split among the players and the right to "blow smoke in the faces of the losers."

It was estimated that the Mid-Winter Baseball Association lost between $500 and $800 on the spring, but as the *Tribune* editorial page explained: "Tampa appreciates to the fullest of these [Chicago] newspapermen. They are all booster, both of the Cubs and their training place. A column or two daily under a Tampa dateline in each Chicago newspaper is potent publicity for this city, the benefits of which are beyond estimation." In fact, the Tampa baseball boosters did turn a modest profit the following spring.

The Cubs were sold on Tampa. Doc Semmens, the Cubs' trainer, said the team "has never started the season with better training and better condition. In fact, I don't believe any club has ever had anything like the good weather that we have had for training purposes. I'm more than glad that we're coming back if for no other reason than I have never had so little trouble in my career."

3

THE FIRST GAME

The players appeared to enjoy their first year in the Tampa Bay area, with reports that at least four decided to adopt Florida as a winter home. On the evening of March 18, 1913, just before the Cubs' special train left for Jacksonville and points north, Murphy signed a five-year extension under nearly the same arrangements as before.

But as it turned out, little else would be the same as before. During the Cubs' first spring in Tampa, Murphy was hounded by reports that other owners in the league wanted him out. Almost exactly eleven months later, on February 21, 1914, Murphy sold the club to lawyer Charles Taft under pressure from Major League Baseball.

Florida was about to see unprecedented growth when it came to its role as a spring training host. A state that had never claimed more than two teams was about to double that number. While the Indians' stay in Florida ended after one spring, the St. Louis Browns moved from Waco, Texas, to St. Petersburg; the Cardinals switched from Columbus, Georgia, to St. Augustine; and the Philadelphia Athletics vacated San Antonio for Jacksonville. "Florida," wrote the *Tampa Tribune*, "has come into favor as a baseball training ground in one year. It was not until the Cubs came to Tampa last year that any serious attention was given Florida in this respect."

The Sunshine State suddenly found itself with more teams that spring than any other state. Tampa Bay had to this point never hosted a game between two major league teams. With the addition of the Browns to St. Pete, local fans were about to see a dozen such games. The Cubs would

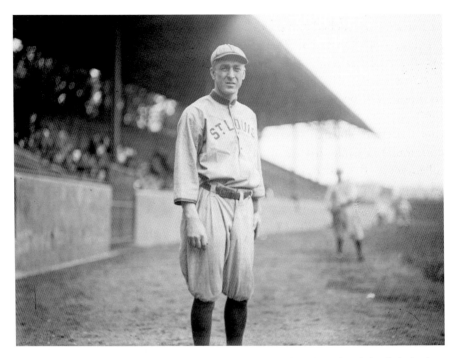

Branch Rickey was the manager of the St. Louis Browns when they played the Cubs in the first major league spring training game in Tampa, in 1914. *Courtesy of Library of Congress.*

play five home games against major league competition; the Browns would play seven.

The very first one came on February 26, when Branch Rickey's Browns crossed Tampa Bay via ferry, a two-hour trip. At the time, water was the preferred route between Tampa and St. Petersburg. As Lopez recalled to Wes Singletary, "Before the Gandy Bridge was built (in 1924), we used to take Memorial Highway and go up around Clearwater and Largo, just to get to St. Pete. It was about sixty miles and a terrible drive. Memorial Highway was just one-lane pavement. If another car was coming from the other direction, you would have to slow down and give him half of the road."

According to Bob Addie of *The Sporting News*, the players often entertained themselves on those ferry rides by feeding the encircling seagulls. "Like all good red-blooded American boys," wrote Addie, "the ballplayers would take some bread aboard and see who had the strongest arm by tossing a piece in the air to the birds. There was one incident, however. Mickey Grasso, a [Senators] catcher with a great arm, won those ferry-crossing contests every time, but he threw his arm out. What a way to go."

The Browns reached Tampa an hour before the 3:00 p.m. affair. Fans could purchase tickets, priced at $0.50 for general admission, $0.75 for grandstand and $1.50 for box seats, or they could watch the game from their car.

It was a Thursday, and businesses were closed in celebration. There were two thousand spectators on hand as Cubs center fielder Cy Williams, in his third of what would be nineteen major league seasons, had a hand in all runs scored in Chicago's 3–2 win. The Notre Dame grad singled, doubled and homered while driving in all 3 runs. His first-inning, 2-run home run rolled across the racetrack in right field far from home plate. He added a run-scoring double in the eighth, but it was his throwing error in the ninth that allowed both of the Browns' runs to score, spoiling a combination shutout by Elmer Koestner and Zip Zabel, who neglected to back up third on Williams's wild throw.

In the spring finale, the Cubs may have experienced their finest moment in Tampa as they shut out Connie Mack's Philadelphia A's, 3–0, while allowing only a single to the World Champions. The win enabled the Cubs to take two of three from Mack's men. Cubs hurlers Larry Cheney and Hippo Vaughn, who would both go on to win 20 games during the regular season, combined to face only twenty-eight batters. In five innings, Cheney allowed only a walk to A's shortstop Larry Kopf, who was quickly erased on a double play. Vaughn worked the final four innings and surrendered a seventh-inning, opposite-field single to second baseman Rube Oldring.

Over the next two springs, all seemed well, except for the fact that the Cubs had not finished in the first division of the National League since landing in Tampa. During the first week of the team's 1916 spring camp, the Tampa

Right-hander George Washington "Zip" Zabel pitched the final four innings to preserve the Cubs' 3–2 win over the Browns in the first major league spring training game played in Tampa, in 1914. *Courtesy of Library of Congress.*

Rotary Club declared, "Our Cubs will not go pennant-less this year," and presented new owner Charles Weeghman, a Chicago restaurateur, with a "pennant" of their own proclaiming the Cubs "Hillsborough Champs" in a gesture of goodwill.

When the Cubs broke camp on March 29, 1916, ending their twenty-three-day stay, only one other National League club had a longer affiliation with its current city. "The team's players and newspapermen all expressed themselves in the most enthusiastic terms regarding the advantages of the city, and are looking forward to their returns next year," wrote the *Tampa Tribune*.

But on October 19, without warning, Weeghman announced that the club would train in Pasadena, California, the following spring. Days later, it was revealed that William Wrigley Jr., one of the directors of the team, was a winter resident of the Rose Bowl City. By 1918, with Weeghman's lunch counter business in decline, Wrigley would become the majority investor of the team. It would remain under his family's control until 1981.

4

WALLOP STUPENDOUS

In 1950, the Associated Press named its two greatest athletes of the first half of the century. Olympian and all-around athlete Jim Thorpe was ranked first, and baseball legend Babe Ruth was second. Both superstars were at Plant Field on April 4, 1919, and yet it was only a footnote because of what else happened that day.

Thorpe had already won two Olympic gold medals and played in both the National Football League and the major leagues. Ruth was about to become the "Sultan of Swat" after five years with the Red Sox as one of the game's most dominating pitchers.

On that sunny Friday afternoon cooled by a morning downpour, Babe Ruth gave Tampa its most celebrated major league moment when he crushed what was likely the longest home run of his career in World Champion Boston's 5–3 win over the New York Giants in front of 4,200 fans. Although there exist varying reports describing the prodigious poke, the *Tampa Tribune* noted that the ball "hit the far edge of the race track and bounded far over into the front yard of the Tampa Bay Hotel."

Frederick Lieb, part of the press corps covering the Giants, was there that day. "The ball never rose more than 30 feet off the ground, but kept going and going. Ross Youngs the right fielder rode out with it until he looked like a small boy chasing after a sparrow."

Ruth's second-inning home run—in his first plate appearance at Plant against major league competition—came off Giants' right-hander "Columbia George" Smith. Aside from being one of only fourteen Columbia University alumni to play in the major leagues, his only other claim to fame is his career winning percentage of .325 (39-81), which presently ranks tied for the third worst in major league history among pitchers with 100 or more decisions.

Wrote *Tampa Tribune* sports editor Gilbert Freeman: "Wallop stupendous, or punch extraordinary, if one would lapse for an instant into the lingo of this squared circle, is what beat the Gotham Giants yesterday afternoon for Babe Ruth's tremendous hoist to the race track in right center in the second stanza jarred the big town bunch away from any grip they might have had on the game and though they stuck at their job to the finish, they couldn't get up and Tampa's Boston Red Sox gathered the first game of the series 5 to 3 while the hugest baseball gathering that has ever thronged Plant Field rooted in real style for the world's champions."

Years later, the *Tribune*'s iconic columnist-editor Tom McEwen observed, "Freeman was attempting to match Ruth by writing the longest sentence in history." Giants Hall of Fame manager John McGaw said after the game, "I believe it is the longest hit I ever saw." At the time, McGraw was in his twenty-eighth year of pro ball.

Estimates of the distance of the blast ranged anywhere from 550 to 587 feet; the latter is the distance listed on the state historical marker located there today. The *Boston Globe*'s Melville Webb Jr. measured the distance the following day. Covering the distance in 179 strides of slightly more than a yard each, the Red Sox beat writer calculated the blast as certainly better than 540 feet.

It was the only home run Ruth would hit at Plant Field in five career games against major league competition, but it had a significant impact on Red Sox manager Ed Barrow. Wrote Lieb of *The Sporting News*: "Barrow decided then that a fellow with such punch should play every day and that Ruth's future career was as a hitter. Barrow pitched Ruth enough in 1919 for him to win eight decisions and lose five, but gradually Ed kept the big fellow in left field against all types of pitching."

On April 2, Ruth pitched his only inning at Plant Field, working one perfect inning with a strikeout for the "Yannigans" in an intrasquad game. During the 1919 season, as he began his journey of becoming the Bambino, Ruth played in 110 games in the outfield, almost twice as many as he ever had before. He went on to hit 29 home runs, one of four times he set the major league season record, breaking his own mark on three occasions. The following January, Ruth was sold by Boston owner Harry Frazee to the Yankees, who quickly became the first team to reach one million in home attendance, drawing three times more than the Red Sox.

Days before Babe Ruth's historic home run at Plant Field on April 4, 1919, fifty-six-year-old former major leaguer, then evangelist Billy Sunday worked out with the Red Sox. Shown are Manager Ed Barrow (*left*), Sunday (*center*) and Ruth. *SABR-Rucker Photo Archives photo.*

Twenty-nine years after the famous shot, the *New York Times* may have resolved the discrepancies in the actual distance with this account: "Ross Youngs [Giants right fielder] pursued the blast as far as the race track and a guard, who was protecting the outfield fences against gate crashers, marked the spot where it landed with a pile of stones. Some extremely curious writers later borrowed a steel tape from the boss carpenter in charge of the construction work there. They measured from the plate to the stones and the tape showed the incredible distance of 552 feet, 8 inches."

The ball was given to former National League outfielder-turned-evangelist Billy Sunday, who was hosting a tent revival on the fairgrounds and who had thrown out the game's ceremonial first pitch. Earlier in the week, Ruth had connected on a ball that hit the track and bounced into the tent, interrupting a sermon.

According to Billy Werber, a former teammate of Ruth's, the Bambino was also on the wrong end of a "shot" in Tampa. Werber told HBO in its 2019 documentary on the Bambino that the womanizing Ruth broke off a relationship with a young woman from Ybor City, and she took her revenge by shooting him in the leg with a revolver from her purse. Werber said Ruth suffered only a flesh wound and laughed it off, calling the shooter a "nice gal," but the scar just below his left calf remained. While the year of the

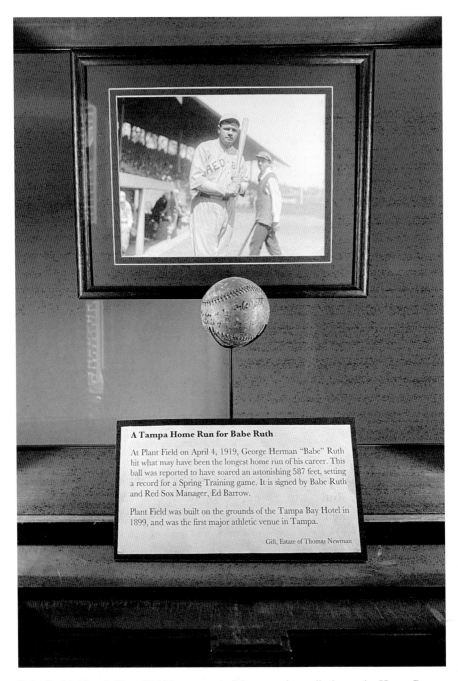

A Tampa Home Run for Babe Ruth

At Plant Field on April 4, 1919, George Herman "Babe" Ruth hit what may have been the longest home run of his career. This ball was reported to have soared an astonishing 587 feet, setting a record for a Spring Training game. It is signed by Babe Ruth and Red Sox Manager, Ed Barrow.

Plant Field was built on the grounds of the Tampa Bay Hotel in 1899, and was the first major athletic venue in Tampa.

Gift, Estate of Thomas Newman

Babe Ruth's historic Plant Field home run ball is currently on display at the Henry B. Plant Museum in Tampa, a gift from the Estate of Thomas Newman. *Courtesy of the Henry B. Plant Museum.*

assault is unknown, Werber noted that the incident took place at the Temple Terrace Country Club, a Ruth favorite.

Meanwhile, the thirty-one-year-old Thorpe, who played all three outfield positions for the Giants, was in the last of his six major league seasons. He appeared that day as pinch hitter in the ninth inning and reached on an error when Hall of Fame pitcher Herb Pennock threw wildly to first after fielding the Olympian's grounder.

While his baseball career was over, it was not Thorpe's last trip to Plant. On New Year's Day 1926, George Halas's Chicago Bears, starring Red Grange, defeated a team known as the Tampa Cardinals. That squad featured a number of college and pro stars, including Thorpe. Grange's 70-yard fourth-quarter touchdown run closed out the scoring in the Bears' 17–3 win before seven thousand fans in Tampa's first professional football game. Thorpe's fumble in the first quarter led to a Chicago field goal.

Early spring trainings were not lengthy stays, and the Red Sox were in Tampa for only nineteen days in 1919. Ruth was in town for only two weeks, arriving on March 23 following his annual prolonged contract negotiation. The partying Bambino was likely in no hurry to arrive, given that Tampa had officially become "dry" on January 1.

But other than breaking one of his two "pet bats" in his first day on the practice field, the *Globe* wrote that "George Ruth is having the time of his life. The spectators at the park do not miss a move he makes." The *Globe* also noted that Ruth was many pounds overweight and that in his third day of camp he "started off for a half-mile run around Plant's track with teammates [Everett] Scott and [Amos] Strunk after the afternoon session, but lasted only for about 150 yards. The big fellow certainly has a lot of work ahead."

The day after Ruth's historic homer, the Red Sox played their only other major league game in Tampa that spring, winning 10–4 over the Giants in front of 4,400 to close out the two-game series with McGraw's men. The two-day gate receipts were a tidy $5,000. Ruth contributed a pair of singles to Boston's 11-hit assault. Four games had been originally scheduled, but Giants skipper John McGraw canceled two, having seen enough of his ill-prepared club.

The Sox departed for Gainesville via train the next day for a rematch with the Giants, but not before they unanimously voted Tampa as "the greatest place in the South for a spring training camp," according to the *Globe*. While the Boston players loved Tampa and the accommodations, including the clubhouse's new hot-water heater installed that spring, Manager Ed Barrow was critical of the condition of the field.

As a result, the Sox returned to their previous spring home in Hot Springs, Arkansas, for 1920. *The Sporting News* reported that the reason the Red Sox left Arkansas in the first place was because the railroad that ran into that resort town was being rerouted and its tracks would be laid through Majestic Field, where the team had trained since 1912. The Sox returned to another field in Hot Springs, Whittington Park, where they trained through 1923.

But for Tampanians, 1919 signaled that major league baseball was back. After two years without it, Tampa, which replaced the Red Sox with Walter Johnson's Senators in 1920, would host spring training for the next sixty-five years, interrupted only by Major League Baseball's prohibition against spring travel during World War II.

5

THE BIG TRAIN

In February 1925, the Yankees arrived in St. Petersburg for the first of what would be thirty-three springs. New York sportswriters would come to consider it jokingly as the "Discovery of St. Petersburg." Across the bay, Tampa, too, had some celebrating to do.

The previous fall, the Washington Senators won what would be the team's only World Series title when their .300-hitting rookie Earl McNeely rapped a ground ball that struck a pebble and bounced over the head of Giants third baseman Fred Lindstrom for a Game 7, twelfth-inning, walk-off single.

And it was at Plant Field the following spring, on March 14, that the Senators received their just rewards: World Championship medals from Commissioner Kenesaw Mountain Landis in a pregame ceremony. According to the *Tampa Tribune*, the festivities were witnessed by the most people to see a baseball game in the city's history, though no official attendance number was given. The gold, oval-shaped medals, just less than two inches in length, were decorated with crossed bats and a baseball in which was set a large diamond. The back of each medal was inscribed with the player's name and position. (The tradition of winners receiving World Series rings didn't begin on an annual basis until the following year with the Pittsburgh Pirates.)

Present were Colonel Jacob Ruppert, president of the Yankees representing the American League; Hall of Famer Christy Mathewson; humorist and playwright George Ade; Tampa mayor Perry G. Wall; and many heralded sportswriters from the major Northeast cities. "Never in the history of this city has there been so many prominent figures of the sports world gathered at a single event," wrote the *Tampa Tribune*.

Unfortunately, the Boston Braves spoiled the day, as their double play combination of shortstop Dave Bancroft, who would go on to become a Hall of Fame manager, and second baseman–pitcher Red Lucas combined for 7 hits and 5 runs in leading Boston to a 12–10 win in the Nats' worst game of the spring. The *Washington Evening Star* couldn't resist the headline, "No Medals for This."

When the Senators arrived in Tampa in 1920 to begin a ten-year run of spring training, the locals knew what they were getting: a team that had finished above .500 only four times in nineteen seasons yet somehow featured the game's greatest pitcher in Walter Johnson, who was riding a streak of ten consecutive 20-win seasons.

But owner Clark Griffith introduced something else, something new to spring training cities: creative marketing.

At their first game at Plant Field, there was none other than Johnson, the "Big Train" himself, in the stands serving as an usher with Griffith's blessing. In 1924, borrowing an idea from Branch Rickey, the Nats introduced to Tampanians the "Knothole Gang," which allowed kids under ten to be admitted free to all home games. He initiated a plan to encourage the city's five largest civic clubs to each "sponsor" a home game and reward the club with the largest attendance with a silver cup.

According to the National Baseball Hall of Fame, "Griffith was known for his desire to entertain the fans. As manager, he hired coaches Nick Altrock and Al Schacht—well known as baseball's funny men—to perform comedy routines on the field between innings," which they did often at Plant Field. It was not unusual to see one or both men walking the foul lines with balancing poles as if they were walking on a high wire, or shooting craps on the field with dice that were a foot square.

Griffith had one other notable distinction aside from being in the Baseball Hall of Fame. He remains the only man in major league history to have been

Members of the Senators break open a crate of Florida oranges during practice at Plant Field. *Courtesy of Tampa-Hillsborough County Public Library System.*

a professional player, manager and owner for at least twenty years apiece. That many-sided experience showed.

The Senators attracted the largest baseball crowds Plant Field had ever seen. As a result, Griffith signed a five-year deal with the city in 1923, and officials responded in kind. *The Sporting News* observed, "The obsolete stands and clubhouse formerly used by the Tampa team have been replaced by a $35,000 steel and concrete grandstand which will seat 4,000 and additional seats for 1,500 have been constructed." Numerous upgrades were also made to the clubhouse."

Johnson, meanwhile, found hard luck in his eight Tampa springs. All told, the Big Train made just seven starts against major league competition at Plant Field and won only twice. In the spring of 1921, coming off a season in which he made only fifteen starts due to a sore arm, he was ineffective and on Opening Day lasted only four innings, the first time he failed to finish a home opener. In 1922, after deciding to make spring training a vacation for the family, both Johnson and his wife, Hazel, took sick. Johnson missed a week of workouts with influenza. Hazel was hospitalized in Tampa and underwent serious sinus surgery at Gordon Keller Memorial Hospital (an ancestor of Tampa General Hospital) near the grounds of the Tampa Bay Hotel. So upset was he over his wife's medical condition and dealing with his own bout of influenza that Johnson was unable to prepare properly for the coming season, and his string of ten consecutive Opening Day starts came to an end. In 1925, Johnson strained his right calf jogging around the Plant Field track. (He often conducted this exercise with a medicine ball.) He was limited to one appearance all spring. And, in 1927, his last as a player, he suffered a broken left ankle when struck by a line drive off the bat of his roommate, Joe Judge, during batting practice on March 9. The injury kept him from pivoting, and he pitched in only eighteen games that season.

On March 28, 1925, in front in front of another huge gathering at Plant Field, the Giants and Senators staged a rematch of Game 1 of the World Series featuring lineups that were exactly the same. In his only appearance of the spring due to his calf injury, Johnson pitched three innings and left trailing, 3–1. After the Nats tied it in the eighth, New York won it with 2 runs in the ninth off another Hall of Famer, Stan Coveleski. Hack Wilson, one of twelve future Hall of Famers to play in the game, tripled in the winning run.

Johnson would make only two more starts against major league opponents at Plant Field. His last, on March 27, 1926, was his best. He worked five innings and allowed only 4 hits and 1 run against John McGraw's Giants with seven future Hall of Famers.

The following year, their first camp without Johnson, the Senators brought sixteen pitchers to camp, all but two under the age of thirty. Through the first quarter of the season, the Nats were 14-27 and allowed a league-high 239 runs. They never recovered.

As a result, Griffith fired Harris and brought back Johnson to manage the team. One month into the 1929 spring season, local trouble started. On March 19, Griffith told city officials that "more suitable arrangements" must be made to ensure the return of the Senators for any more springs. At the center of the issue was a conflict between the Nats and the hometown minor league Smokers over the use of the field.

Plant Field was indeed a busy place. According to Joe Falls of *The Sporting News*, in the spring of 1928, future Hall of Famer Goose Goslin noticed a shotput left behind by one of the high school track teams that also practiced there. He picked it up and gave it a heave, only to tear a muscle in his shoulder. Blessed with a rifle arm, Goose was unable to put much behind his throws all spring.

Tampa dropped out of the Florida State League in 1928. When they returned the following year in the Class B Southeastern League, they sought practice space at Plant Field.

Above: Senators take pregame batting practice on Plant Field's "game" field. The sign in center field marks the exit for "Negroes." *Tampa Bay History Center photo.*

Opposite: Tampa mayor Perry G. Wall takes in a Senators game at Plant Field in 1926. *Courtesy of Tampa-Hillsborough County Public Library System.*

The issue went unresolved through the summer until, according to *The Sporting News*, the chamber of commerce sent Griffith the following telegram on September 24, 1929: "Understanding you were moving the Washington Club from Tampa. Opened negotiations with the Detroit club and closed with it this afternoon. Sincerely trust you find satisfactory quarters elsewhere." Bucky Harris, who had just completed his first year piloting the Tigers, confessed that he pleaded acceptance when the Tigers received the offer from Tampa city officials.

In early November, Griffith announced that his team was headed for Biloxi, Mississippi, where they would train for six years, officially ending their ten-year Tampa run.

MARCH 23, 1920. The World Champion Cincinnati Reds beat the Senators, 6–4. Walter Johnson, who had already won 297 games by the age of thirty-one, pitched four innings, and Cuban legend Dolf Luque, who would go on to win 194 games, worked five. Neither pitcher figured in the decision. Reds Hall of Fame center fielder Edd Roush hauled in Judge's long fly ball in center for the last out.

MARCH 17, 1923. Christening a new 4,000-seat grandstand, the Nats lost to the Braves, 24–12, in front of 4,500, largest crowd to see the Nats in Tampa. Washington pitchers surrendered 26 hits and were hurt by 9 errors.

MARCH 15, 1924. Approximately 1,300 fans turned out in frigid weather on Board of Trade Day as the Senators defeated the Braves, 10–6. Casey Stengel had 3 hits for the Braves, and Goose Goslin went 3-for-3 with 2 walks for the hosts.

MARCH 5, 1927. The Senators' newest addition, Tris Speaker, made his Plant Field debut and delivered a pinch-hit single in a 9–6 loss to Braves. Speaker, who batted .380 or better five times, was in the next-to-last season of his twenty-two-year career.

MARCH 19, 1927. The Nats lost to Hall of Famer Burleigh Grimes and the Giants, 5–4 as another Hall of Famer, Rogers Hornsby, threw out the tying run at the plate from second base in the ninth inning.

MARCH 29–31, 1927. The Nats swept a three-game series from the World Champion Cardinals. On Tuesday, with two out and the bases loaded in the ninth inning, Earl McNeely singled to tie the game and Stuffy Stewart walked to give the Senators a 3–2 win over the Cardinals. The Nats won another close game on Wednesday, 5–4, and followed it up on Thursday with another walk-off, winning 5–4 on a double by journeyman outfielder Nick Cullop.

MARCH 12, 1929. The Yankees beat the Southeastern Class B League's Smokers, 1–0, in Babe Ruth's return to Plant Field. He and Gehrig combined to go 0-for-7.

MARCH 26, 1929. Tampa's Al Lopez wore a major league uniform in Tampa for the first time as he caught for the Brooklyn Robins in the first game of a two-game series against the Senators. Lopez had 2 singles in the Robins' 7–6 loss. He would go on to spend the entire season with the Atlanta Crackers in the Southern Association.

6

WALL STREET CRASH
HAD TAMPA SEEING RED(S)

Before they could begin what would be an unprecedented six-decade relationship with the City of Tampa, the Reds stubbed their toe. Literally.

Walking on the sand at Palm Beach a few days before the team was to report to Tampa in the spring of 1931, Reds manager Dan Howley injured his toe. "Infection has set in," wrote the *Tampa Tribune*. "While the injury is not serious, attending physicians advised him against driving over to Tampa until later in the week."

Some eighteen months earlier, in 1929, auto executive Sydney Weil purchased the Reds only weeks before Wall Street crashed. Not long after, *The Sporting News* quoted him as saying, "The present financial condition of the Cincinnati club is such that every dollar which can be saved, must be saved." While it was a difficult realization for the thirty-nine-year-old, second-year owner, it was the effect of the Great Depression that played a role in the Reds' move to Tampa.

Seeking "economy and efficiency," Weil announced that the Reds would move from their previous spring site in Orlando to Tampa. Wrote *The Sporting News*, "The hotel rate obtained there [Tampa] for the players is less than what the club has been in the habit of paying in Orlando, there will be no transportation costs for getting the players to and from the ball park as that is only a couple of blocks from the Tampa Bay Hotel, and on top of this, the prospect of drawing good crowds to the exhibition games is better than in the town the Reds are leaving after eight years." *The Sporting News*

During their time in Tampa, the Reds stayed at all three hotels shown: the Tampa Terrace (*right*), the Hillsborough Hotel (*left*) and the Floridan, seen in the distance. *Courtesy of Tampa-Hillsborough County Public Library System.*

estimated the cost savings to be approximately $6,000, an extraordinary sum in those desperate times.

The weather that first spring, according to the *Cincinnati Enquirer*, was Tampa's worst in forty-one years. The Reds won only three of fifteen games, including only one at Plant Field, although it came against the Cardinals' Hall of Famer Dizzy Dean. Reds infielder Frank Sigafoos, who played for four teams in his three-season career and never hit a home run in the regular season, hit a deep fly to center field off Dean that bounced on the surrounding racetrack and bounded behind the scoreboard for a home run, breaking a 5–5 tie in the seventh.

Howley summed up his thoughts on the spring with a candid assessment in the March 31 *Tampa Tribune*: "I am not in the least discouraged by our wretched showing in the games played so far. I am perfectly willing to admit that the team at present is just about the worst looking major league outfit that I have ever seen. There is no defying the plain fact that we have practically no punch and that the defense has faltered mainly through the nervousness and over anxiety of the boys on account of their inability to hit. But I am positive that there are better times coming. I firmly believe that the team has gotten the worst of its efforts out of its system and will show a steady improvement from now on."

The next spring didn't start out better, as Tampa mayor Robert E. Lee Chauncey announced that the city-owned Tampa Bay Hotel would have to close at the end of the year if financial obligations weren't met. Under the strain of the Great Depression, they weren't. For the first time, a team training in Tampa wouldn't be staying at the Tampa Bay Hotel. The Reds instead lodged at the Hillsborough Hotel for the spring of 1933 before eventually moving to the still-standing Floridan.

And so it went. The Reds would post a losing regular season record in their first seven springs in Tampa, average ninety-two losses a season and burn through four different managers. The Depression severely affected Tampa's baseball community. The Reds drew only 556 fans in the 1933 spring finale, an 8–5 win over the Braves, and only 3,649 fans showed for their five games.

On the other hand, while prices for many goods and services fell significantly, it cost the Reds only five dollars a day to lodge, board and train each player during March 1933, two dollars less than the year before.

Meanwhile, Weil's other business interests eventually went under, and in November 1933, he surrendered control of the Reds after reportedly losing more than $600,000.

A few weeks before they opened camp in 1934, the Reds were purchased by radio manufacturer Powel Crosby Jr. When the team assembled in Tampa for their first workout, Crosley flew up from his winter home in Sarasota to inspect the troops. His seaplane landed in the nearby Hillsborough River and was moored to the seawall.

In one of Crosley's first acts, he renamed the Reds' home park in Cincinnati from Redland Field to Crosley Field. Another of his early moves was to hire the brilliant but capricious future Hall of Fame executive Larry MacPhail as general manager. The Society for American Baseball Research wrote about him: "Flamboyant, visionary, ego—or monomaniacal, tempestuous, alcoholic, and self-destructive—the words approach but do not satisfactorily explain Larry MacPhail. He was a mover and shaker in the world of Major League Baseball."

The Reds were the first of three organizations MacPhail would help turn around with his revolutionary ideas. Under MacPhail, the Reds became the first team to host night games, the first to broadcast their spring games on the radio and the first to travel by plane. And during his three-year tour with the Reds, he began to set the table for wins. But it wasn't going to be easy, and it wasn't going to be conventional.

The Reds brought fifty-one players to Tampa in 1934, their most ever. Among the group was Tampa's own Al Lopez, a holdout at Dodgers camp who worked out with the Reds. Still unsigned, Lopez was in the stands wearing a brown suit at Plant on March 22 when the Dodgers visited the Reds. Lopez's replacement, Luke Sukeforth, committed a throwing error in the first inning that led to a run in Brooklyn's 3–2 loss. Lopez accompanied the Dodgers back to Orlando after the game and signed for a reported $10,000 the next day.

Paul Derringer, who lost 27 games in 1933 but who would become a six-time all-star, started the Reds' spring opener against the World Champion Giants. Baseball reared its unpredictable head: The Reds won, 14–7, Derringer earned the win and a season-high 3,500 attended.

MacPhail worked closely with Tampa Chamber of Commerce chairman Frank M. Traynor on a big push to sell tickets. The team lowered prices, including twenty-five-cent tickets for schoolchildren, and revived the Knothole Gang.

On March 25 at Plant Field, the Reds held reigning Triple Crown winner Jimmie Foxx to a single in defeating seventy-one-year-old Connie Mack's Philadelphia A's, 5–1. "Both teams passed the hat among the customers during the game seeking dimes for a memorial to the late John McGraw, Connie's only rival in baseball fame," stated the *Tribune*. McGraw had died one month earlier.

At the end of the spring season, MacPhail also made a bold promise: The Reds wouldn't require a cash guarantee to return in 1935, asking, according to the *Tribune*, only that "some group of Tampans sponsor, direct and take charge of ticket sales. The reason we want some Tampa group to take charge is that you people here are more familiar with the situation. We want your interest and cooperation. We stand ready to book a dozen exhibition games with big league clubs for 1935 right this moment so that the Tampa group can map out its program months ahead."

Reds manager Chuck Dressen, in his first major league camp, may have provided one of the early signs of analytics. "A record is kept at each batting practice session of the number of bad balls at which each batter swings," observed *The Sporting News*. "Dressen shows this record to each man guilty of biting at the bad ones and coaches them of getting out of that habit."

Another of those experiencing his first spring camp in 1935 was Walter Lanier "Red" Barber, a future Hall of Famer, who MacPhail had hired a year earlier as the team's first radio broadcaster. The twenty-seven-year-old Barber began his broadcasting career as a student on the University of Florida radio station. When Crosley purchased the Reds, the team became more radio conscious, and Barber talked his way into a job. While he had played plenty of sandlot baseball, the first major league game he saw was his first day on the job with the Reds. That spring, the redhead was running all over Plant Field, taping daily interviews with players that were heard

Left: Reds pitcher Johnny Vander Meer instructing Tampa-area high school students at Plant Field. *Courtesy of Florida Photograph Collection.*

Right: Hall of Fame broadcaster Red Barber, a University of Florida graduate, handled radio play-by-play for the Reds in the 1930s. Here, he is calling a game from Plant Field on Tampa's WDAE Radio. *Public domain.*

locally in Tampa on WDAE radio and on WLW, the Reds' flagship and the country's first superstation. Barber was also behind the mic for one of Tampa's most talked-about events: Babe Ruth's first game as a Brave in the Reds' spring opener on March 9.

The thirty-plus sportswriters covering the game sent approximately thirty thousand words to newspapers in many cities. The *Tampa Tribune* reported that there were "more newspapermen gathered in the press box to report how the big fellow looked in a Boston Braves uniform than ever before gathered in one spot in Tampa."

The Associated Press wrote that Ruth looked "a bit strange at first base in the red and gray uniform of the Braves, but otherwise resembled the same old Babe in all his portly glory."

After joking with Reds bespectacled right-handed starter Danny MacFayden, a former Yankees teammate, before his first at bat, Ruth stepped into the box and lined the first pitch he saw into right field for an RBI single, his only hit of the day. There were some 3,500 fans in attendance for the Braves' 5–3 win over the Reds.

The two teams met again the next day, and the Reds hammered out 22 hits, winning 12–2 while holding Ruth hitless in three at bats. The highlight of the day was a handshake and apology from the St. Louis Cardinals' twenty-five-year-old ace, Dizzy Dean, to Ruth. The two had mixed it up in the press earlier in the spring, and Dean made the trip from the Cardinals camp in Bradenton to apologize.

Dean was back at Plant three weeks later, and although he didn't pitch in the Cardinals' 8–3 victory, he caused another stir as only a flaky, uninhibited thirty-game winner can. After warming up before the game on the practice mound between third base and the grandstand, Dean wandered through the 1,149 customers, glad-handing his numerous acquaintances there.

(Dean often found the glare of the spotlight on and off the field, and Tampa was no exception. It was at the Tampa Terrace Hotel in 1937 that "Ole Diz" got into a public dustup with Jack Miley, the hefty columnist from the *New York Daily News*. It was widely reported that Dean, spurred on by Mrs. Dean and still in his uniform following a game with the Reds, struck the writer in the head with his baseball spikes.)

In what would be his last spring with the Reds, MacPhail had another new idea for training his team in 1936. On February 6, the Reds left New York Harbor via luxury liner to Puerto Rico, where they would play a series of exhibition games, becoming the first major league team in organized ball to visit the island. The Reds also stopped in the Dominican Republic. It was all groundbreaking but met with skepticism, as evidenced by the headline in *The Sporting News* of January 20: "Reds' Long Jaunt Defies Logic" But, the publication added, "They again have shown the way to other major league clubs and if they're long journeying brings them at last to the flag, they may start a vogue that someday is likely to find some club training in Japan."

The Reds arrived in Tampa via plane from the Caribbean on March 10 to begin a schedule of thirty-plus exhibition games. On touchdown, MacPhail proclaimed: "The club is in fine condition. We were careful not to overwork the players in Puerto Rico and as a result they are in good shape for the tough series of exhibition games we have arranged for them."

The Reds pitched their way to the second-best record in the Grapefruit League, and it carried all the way through to September 10, when they were two games over .500. MacPhail's men, however, ran out of gas on their final road trip, perhaps the result of so much preseason activity. Still, their seventy-four wins were their most since training in Tampa.

While the Reds made much progress on and off the field under MacPhail, his erratic behavior was too much for Crosley to bear. On November 1, Warren Giles, a future National League president and Hall of Famer, succeeded MacPhail.

Meanwhile, the optimistic Dressen told writer Si Burick in the spring of 1937: "We've got the best rookie camp in Florida. No foolin. I'm like the old woman in the shoe, I've got so many good players I don't know what to do. Know what? We can take it all."

Left: Reds intrasquad game at Plant Field. *Courtesy of Tampa-Hillsborough County Public Library System*.

Below: The Pepsi Cola Giants were one of the many Tampa Bay–area semiprofessional baseball teams that featured some of the best Black ballplayers of the 1930s and 1940s. *Courtesy of Tampa Baseball Museum*.

They didn't, and Dressen was fired a few months later in the middle of what would be a ninety-eight-loss season. Giles hired future Hall of Fame manager Bill McKechnie as his new skipper. At $25,000 a year, he became the third-highest-paid manager, behind the two New York skippers, Bill Terry and Joe McCarthy.

McKechnie was known for getting the most out of his pitchers. In 1941, while leading the reigning World Series Champions, he took only twelve to camp. Al Lopez said of him, "He handled pitchers better than anybody I ever saw."

The Reds were set up for success, and they had the right man at the helm.

MARCH 14, 1931. The Yankees beat the Reds, 6–5, as Ruth contributed an RBI single and Gehrig hit 2 doubles in front of 1,500. Ruth threw two dozen autographed baseballs into the stands to orphans from the Tampa Children's Home and the Catholic orphanage who were guests of Sidney Weil, president of the Cincinnati ballclub.

MARCH 29, 1933. Red Sox outfielder Johnny Watwood went 6-for-6 with 5 singles, 1 double, 2 RBI and, strangely, no runs in Boston's 10–4 win over the Reds. During the regular season, Watwood had only 4 hits in 30 at bats.

MARCH 23, 1934. The Reds beat the bearded House of David, 8–7, on a bases-loaded walk in the bottom of the ninth at Plant Field. House of David pitcher Mike Janesko charged the umpire on the final pitch. Wrote the *Tampa Tribune*: "Grabbing his whiskers with one hand to keep them from dragging on the ground, Mr. Janesko raced over to umpire Johnston and in no soft tones, offered to buy him a pair of spectacles. Fortunately, a half dozen policemen stepped in and settled the argument."

APRIL 8, 1934. In their spring finale in Tampa, the Reds lost to the Cardinals' Dizzy and Paul Dean, 2–1. Dizzy worked the first six innings and Paul the final three to earn the win before three thousand fans.

MARCH 22, 1935. Giants future Hall of Fame right fielder Mel Ott hit his first Plant Field home run, a 2-run poke in the first inning as the New York Giants beat the Reds, 6–5.

MARCH 15, 1936. Boston's Jimmie Foxx hit a 460-foot home run, but the Reds prevailed, 13–8. The blow cleared the center-field wall and landed on the racetrack.

MARCH 19, 1937. A few days after signing his contract ending a brief holdout, twenty-two-year-old Joe DiMaggio made his Plant Field debut as a pinch-hitter in the Yankees' 7–3 loss to the Reds in the spring opener. He popped up to short right field. DiMaggio earned the World Champions' biggest raise that spring, going from $6,500 to $15,000. He arrived at Yankees camp that morning and made the trip to Tampa with his teammates.

MARCH 31, 1937. The Reds trailed the Boston Bees, 10–1, after six innings but rallied to win, 11–10. Future Hall of Famer Ernie Lombardi's single in the bottom of the ninth won it. Reds pitchers walked 17 batters. Johnny Vander Meer earned the win. Only 224 fans saw it.

MARCH 20, 1938. The Reds' first Latin America Day saw the hosts win their fifth straight, 2–1, over the Red Sox. Miss Lydia Palenzuela, Latin America Beauty Queen for 1938, threw out the first pitch while 1,600 observed.

GRAPEFRUIT LEAGUE'S FIRST NO-HITTER SAVED BY APPEAL

At the Reds' 1939 home opener on March 12, Reds right-handers Whitey Moore and Gene Thompson combined to throw Plant Field's only Grapefruit League no-hitter and what was believed to be the first in league history in besting Leo Durocher's Dodgers, 5–0, before 2,800 fans.

Dodgers second baseman Pete Coscarart's baserunning blunder in the first inning made the gem possible. Coscarart hit a line drive to right field and reached second base but was called out after the Reds appealed to umpire George Magerkurth that he missed first base. As a result, the base hit was taken away from Coscarart. (According to Dirk Lammers from nonohitters.com, only once in major league history has there been a no-hitter saved by an appeal play: September 7, 1923, when the Red Sox's Howard Ehmke was credited with a no-hitter when his A's mound counterpart, Slim Harris, also missed first base after hitting a pseudo double.) Moore hurled the first six innings and Thompson the final three. The game ended when Cincinnati's four-time all-star left fielder Wally Berger hauled in a long drive off the bat of former Yankee Tony Lazzeri, who was in the last year of a Hall of Fame career.

APRIL 3, 1938. In the home finale, the Reds dropped a 7–2 decision to the Cardinals' Gashouse Gang as Cards third baseman Pepper Martin hit a home run, 2 triples and a single and drove in 3 runs before the largest crowd of the year at 2,185. Sammy Baugh entered the game as a defensive replacement at shortstop in the ninth. Baugh had just completed his first season as quarterback of the 1937 NFL Champion Washington Redskins.

MARCH 10, 1940. During a 7-run seventh inning, Red Sox rookie Dominic DiMaggio injured his ankle while scoring from second on a single by Ted Williams. DiMaggio was trying to beat the throw from his brother, Vince, the Reds' right fielder, and collided with teammate John Peacock, who was casually strolling to the plate from third. Both runners were safe, as the Red Sox won, 13–10. Each brother singled and tripled in the game.

MARCH 29, 1940. In their last home game of the spring, the Reds fell to the Tigers, 10–8. Hank Greenberg had 2 singles, a double and a home run and drove in 3 runs. Then, 186 days later, the two met again in the World Series. The Reds prevailed in seven games.

7

TAMPA'S ALL-STAR MOMENT

The first official Major League Baseball All-Star Game was held in 1933 and has been hosted by thirty-seven teams in fifty-seven different ballparks since. It's been a long wait to host one for the Tampa Bay Rays and Tropicana Field—the longest, in fact. No team or ballpark has gone longer without welcoming the Midsummer Classic.

Long before either the existence of the team or the Trop, however, Tampa Bay did indeed host a major league All-Star Game, and it was a Tampa native who scored the deciding run in a walk-off win. *The Sporting News* called it the "best of All Star games, tighter and more dramatic than any of the [previous] regular All-Star Games. There were no fat World Series slices or diamond studded trinkets for the winners, but each fought as hard as though a big World Series check hung in the balance."

"For a day," wrote the *Tampa Tribune*'s Bill Abbott, "it made Tampa the sports capital of the world sending out more than 90,000 words of vivid accounts and descriptions by sixty top-notch writers, hundreds of photographs and miles of movie film."

And even though it was eighty-four years ago, the circumstances surrounding the game were eerily similar to today; the news headlines were nearly interchangeable.

The Russian army had just crossed its border and unleashed a devastating attack on a smaller, vulnerable country. Their bombs left many homeless. The attack was condemned by the League of Nations, forerunner to the United Nations, which expelled Russia. The U.S. president warned against

The promotional flyer for Tampa's 1940 All-Star Game as prepared by the local Peninsular Advertising Agency. Tampa Tribune *photo*.

bombing civilians. And the smaller army not only held on; it also inflicted surprising damage to Stalin's powerful Red Army. Known as the Winter War, it began on November 30, 1939, when Finland fell under a devasting Russian blitz from air, land and sea.

The following month, the United States reacted to the atrocity by forming the Finnish Relief Fund under the direction of former president Herbert Hoover. At a meeting of Hoover and New York City sportswriters at the Waldorf-Astoria Hotel the following January 4, a special sports committee was formed with the intention of raising money during the first quarter of the year for the relief fund. Those representing baseball, golf, basketball, track, horse racing, boxing, polo and hockey all pledged their support and agreed to work with their sports leaders to assist in fundraising.

New York World-Telegram columnist Joe Williams chaired the sports committee, and Dan Daniel of the same paper was the baseball representative. He approached major league baseball officials about hosting a fundraising opportunity during spring training, and the group agreed on the idea of an all-star game between the best players from the six National League teams and five American League teams training in Florida.

Miami, St. Petersburg and Tampa were given consideration to host the game, but in the end a baseball diamond wouldn't fit in the Orange Bowl properly, and much to the dismay of St. Pete's tireless ambassador, Al Lang, Waterfront Park in that city was too small and too frail. Plant Field, Tampa's first major athletic venue on the grounds of the Tampa Bay Hotel, had more permanent seats than any ballpark in Florida. It became the favorite among the committee. The announcement was made on Valentine's Day.

The Sporting News declared: "Tampa earned the selection because as a training camp, it is 'The City Which Has Everything' as the chamber of commerce advertises. It [Plant Field] featured the largest clubhouse any big league team uses in Florida, probably anywhere. A huge, high-ceiled room, big enough for a college basketball court, provides plenty of locker space, trunk storage room and is well ventilated. Compared to many other clubhouses, this one is a palace. And the city water here is not only pure and soft, but tastes good."

Sports committee chairman Williams added that the city had something else going for it. "Tampa was chosen for the game because of its enthusiasm from the start. When the game was first proposed Mayor [Robert E. Lee] Chancey, the chamber of commerce, the two Tampa newspapers and others began to besiege the committee with telegrams."

Much of the enthusiasm came from Frank Winchell, the publicity director for the Tampa Terrace Hotel, the chairman of the All-Star Game committee and a most enterprising fellow. Four years prior, Winchell had the hotel convert room bathrooms of the sports photographers covering spring training into darkrooms. And it was no accident that seventeen of the first nineteen Annual Governor's Dinners were held at the Tampa Terrace.

Within forty-eight hours of the announcement of the game, Winchell proclaimed to the *Tampa Tribune*, "Almost every city in which a big-league club is located has sent in requests for tickets to the game."

Checks for tickets, priced at $5.00 for box, $2.00 for reserved grandstand, $1.00 for unreserved pavilion seats and $0.50 for unreserved bleachers, began pouring in, many for more than the price of the tickets with the understanding that the leftover be donated to the relief fund. There would be no complimentary tickets. Even the 140 media members who covered the game paid $1.00 for admission. Any visiting players wishing to attend the game and Commissioner Kenesaw Mountain Landis himself would be paying for their tickets.

Patriotism was in the air. Emotions were high. The game was scheduled for March 17. It happened to be St. Patrick's Day as well as Palm Sunday, and it was the same day that Germany's and Italy's leaders, Adolf Hitler and Benito Mussolini, were forging an unholy alliance against France and England at a meeting deep in the Alps of northern Italy. Three days before the game, Russia and Finland had signed a peace treaty, but it didn't matter. Commissioner Landis quickly issued a statement: "It will be the biggest thing ever attempted in a baseball way in Florida and I'm sure it will go over big. The Finns need relief now more than ever." He added, "There is no reason for any changes in plans being made."

Governor Fred Cone declared it Baseball Day in Florida. Mutual Radio announced it would carry the game live nationally and Red Barber would be in the broadcast booth. Tampa's WDAE Radio, two months short of its eighteenth birthday, would cover the game locally with sports director "Salty Sol" Fleischman also describing the action.

Gameday temperatures reached into the seventies, but the sky was drab and overcast. Still, the atmosphere was captivating. Wrote Williams in the *New York World-Telegram*: "The field and stands were liberally sprayed with bunting and flags. It was a strange unfamiliar touch; the blue elongated cross of Finland against a field of white. All over the grounds the Finnish flags fluttered proudly beneath the stars and stripes. Somehow this seemed to be symbolic, a stern, firmly settled democracy hovering protectively over a new and bewildered son of the same political philosophy."

As it did often, the University of Tampa band played pregame. Every seat was filled thirty minutes before game time, with many of those seated dressed in honor of Ireland's patron saint. In the first row behind home plate sat fifty local orphans, guests of Hollywood elites Clark Gable, Vivien Leigh, Ingrid Bergman and Al Jolson among other notables who donated a combined $3,500 to the cause. Joining Commissioner Landis in his box were NL president Ford Frick, his AL counterpart Will Harridge and Captain Felix Lundberg of the Finnish freighter *Solbritt*, anchored at the Port of Tampa. So large was the media contingent that the Plant Field press box had to be expanded to accommodate the throng. The announced crowd of 13,180 was the largest to see a baseball game in Florida history, a distinction that held for sixteen years.

A team of twenty-six baseball writers covering the eleven Grapefruit League teams had selected the all-star rosters, twenty-five to a side. The game featured fifteen future Hall of Famers, and each squad had seventeen players who had either played or would play in an official midsummer extravaganza. Twenty-two players who played in the game would also play as all-stars at Sportsman's Park in St. Louis four months later. A pair of future Hall of Famers who faced off against each other in the World Series only six months before managed the clubs: the Yankees' Joe McCarthy and the Reds' Bill McKechnie. A coin flip determined that the NL would be the home team, which seemed appropriate, given that Plant Field was the home of the senior circuit's Reds.

The American League, with slugging stars Joe DiMaggio, Ted Williams, Jimmie Foxx, Hank Greenberg and Bill Dickey, was heavily favored. The NL was missing two perennial all-stars in future Hall of Fame first baseman Johnny Mize and pitcher Mort Cooper, a pair of Cardinals who were ill and unable to cross the bay from their spring home in St. Petersburg. Five NL pitchers, however, kept the powerful junior loop in check, and the game went into the ninth tied, 1–1. A sensational stop in the fourth inning by Giants three-time all-star shortstop Billy Jurges on a smash by DiMaggio with a runner on third base kept it that way.

After the Giants' eighteen-game winner Harry Gumbert retired the American Leaguers in order in the top of the inning, NL catcher and Ybor City's Al Lopez led off the bottom of the ninth with a single to center field off the game's premier pitcher at the time, Bob Feller, who would go on to win twenty-seven games for the Indians that year. Cardinals center fielder Terry Moore, a four-time all-star, dropped a sacrifice bunt to the left side of the infield, and Feller's Indians teammate Hal Trosky at first base was unable to hold on to the throw from catcher Rollie Hemsley as Moore reached safely and Lopez advanced to third. Brooklyn's Pete Coscarart then drilled a hard ground ball off Yankees shortstop Frank Crosetti's glove and through the drawn-in infield, scoring Lopez with the winning run as the NL partisan crowd cheered on their favorite son.

United Press sports editor Harry Ferguson wrote about the postgame celebration this way: "The wine casks gushed in a triumphant flow in the Spanish settlement of Tampa last night, for Señor Alphonse Lopez turned out to be the hometown boy who made good in the all-star game. Tables were laden with chicken and yellow rice and pompano cooked in paper bags and persons of Spanish descent told stories of how the señor had struck a mighty blow that started the National League off to victory. After years of playing in the major and minor leagues, fate gave Señor Lopez his hour of glory in front of his neighbors, relatives and his bride of a few months. That is why the celebration out in the Spanish section known as Ybor City was going full blast last night and threatening to last until early manana, as the Señor would say."

The 2–1 walk-off win featured only 11 hits—all singles—and was described by *Detroit News* sports editor H.G. Salsinger as an "old-fashioned game decided in an old-fashioned way." So taken with the entire scene was Salsinger that he suggested the official annual All-Star Game be switched from July to March and played in Tampa. "The Tampa game has left the north with something to shoot at," he opined.

Williams summed it up as "the South's most magnificent tribute to baseball and to suffering humanity. Thousands filled the stands and boiled over on the grounds in mass approval of America's most popular sport and in noisy heart-stirred denunciation of dictator savagery. This made it more than just another ballgame, it was a ballgame with tender international implications. The tempo of play and fervor of the crowd reached from palm-fringed Plant Field to gun-shelled Helsinki. It had all the frills and thrills of a World Series setting. Tampa and its neighboring cities did themselves proud in supporting the most elaborate ballgame in the history of the South."

How big was the game for the Cigar City? It was the lead story on page one in the *Tampa Morning Tribune*, which devoted five additional pages of the paper's sixteen-page edition to game coverage. It all added up to nineteen different stories, a play-by-play account of the game and twenty-one photographs.

A day later, the *Tribune* editorial staff wrote, "We are convinced that the spring All-Star game can be made an annual event and we hope to see Judge Landis, the two leagues and the managers and players agree on making it a permanent feature."

A Finnish student named Heinjoke Vuoski drove up from Miami and wrote a column for the *Tribune* about his first baseball game experience: "I am quite puzzled and upset by it because I could not make out the helter-skelter of what went on. It was all confusing, but I like it."

The Finnish relief fund received a check for $21,295 adding to the $2.5 million raised across the nation through the first quarter of 1940. The outcome proved to be a precursor for the official game on July 9 at St. Louis. The NL won, 4–0, limiting the favorites to only 3 hits.

Later that year at Major League Baseball's winter meetings in Chicago, opinions differed as to the lasting value of an all-star game during spring training. The National League was in favor of playing the game, with proceeds going to equip trainee baseball teams. The American League did not agree, and neither did Landis, who cast the deciding ballot. The underlying reason was fear of injuries to players who weren't yet in shape to play in such a competitive contest, a circumstance not unlike what today's owners face with the World Baseball Classic.

The health of the players is, of course, a valid point. Joe DiMaggio, for instance, had not even played in a spring game prior to starting in center field for the American League that memorable day at Plant Field. But to the 13,180 on hand that day, it hardly mattered.

"It is unfortunate a combination of circumstances seems to make it wise to forego what might have become a keenly anticipated fixture of each spring," stated *The Sporting News* in its December 19, 1940 edition. The idea was revisited in 1956 but was again defeated.

8

THE BATBOY

In the spring of 1939, a teenager named Marcelo Maseda showed up at Plant Field hoping to be the batboy for the Cincinnati Reds. He immediately impressed Reds manager Bill McKechnie who told him that beyond the heavy workload that would come with being a batboy, Maseda would have to learn the names of some seventy-five players and coaches and each of their individual equipment needs.

Unwittingly, McKechnie had lit a fuse in the young Tampeño that would burn for a lifetime.

The next morning, the eager youngster walked five miles from his home in West Tampa to begin his dream job. Wanting to impress the Reds' future Hall of Fame manager, Marcelo arrived at 7:00 a.m., an hour early, determined to beat McKechnie to the field that day. "Mr. McKechnie," Marcelo would say years later, "treated me like a son."

Marcelo found that the players, too, were welcoming. By the end of the first day, they had given him a new glove, a Reds cap and baseball cleats, as his positive energy did not go unnoticed.

"Marselo is no ordinary training camp bat snatcher," wrote Tom Swope of the *Cincinnati Post*. "He's a hustling young Latin who became attached to the Reds at their Tampa training base as a batboy and aide to Larry McManus, clubhouse custodian, property man and assistant trainer of the Reds. Marselo worked so hard to do anything and everything possible to help get the Reds into trim for the pennant race that each year the returning members of the Redleg party felt they were 'home' as soon as they saw his

Left: Marcelo Maseda
with Reds manager Bill
McKechnie. *Courtesy of
Marlene Maseda Lee.*

Below: Marcelo Maseda with
Reds three-time twenty-
game winner Bucky Walters.
Courtesy of Marlene Maseda Lee.

smiling face and heard his broken English on the Plant Field diamond or in the clubhouse."

He remained with the Reds into his early twenties, and as a result, friendships were formed with players, some of whom were only slightly older. Shortstop Eddie Miller and all-star pitchers Bucky Walters and Paul Derringer remained longtime friends. Derringer served as Marcelo's best man.

Some seven decades later, after Marcelo's death in 2012, it was no surprise that local historian Mario Nuñez said this about the former Reds batboy: "He, more than anybody else in Tampa, was regarded as the man that you needed to see. If you wanted to be the mayor of this town, you had to get his blessing. Marcelo was an icon in Tampa's local history. Not only was he Google before we knew what Google was, he also knew everybody and everybody knew him."

"I just liked to help people," Maseda told WUSF's *Tampa Natives Show* in 2011. "I would try and meet ten new people every day." One of those new people was John F. Kennedy. As a two-time alcalde, or unofficial mayor, of Tampa's Ybor City, Maseda presented the president with a special box of cigars on Kennedy's visit to Tampa in 1963, days before he was killed by an assassin's bullet. "My father loved many things," Maseda's daughter Marlene said recently, "but baseball and cigars were tied for number one." As she often was, Marlene was with her father that day. The six-year-old presented the president with a doll from Spain for Kennedy's five-year-old daughter, Caroline.

When he wasn't helping the Reds, Marcelo set baseball and football school records at Jefferson High School. He went on to play minor league baseball for the Tampa Smokers and the Cubs' affiliate in Portsmouth, Virginia. He returned home to go to the University of Tampa, where he served as the student body president and graduated at age thirty-two, according to the *St. Petersburg Times*. He would go on to coach baseball at his college alma mater and for American Legion Post 248 in West Tampa, where he counted Lou Pinella and Tony LaRussa among his players. Richard Stone, a former Democratic U.S. senator from Florida and Florida secretary of state, once hired Maseda as an aide.

But that first spring in 1939 at Plant Field was where it began. "If anyone asked him to do anything he started off on a dead run to do it," wrote Swope.

After giving him $600 and plenty of baseball equipment when their Tampa training stay ended, that first spring the Reds made another offer to Maseda. On clinching their first National League pennant in twenty years, they invited him to join them for the World Series as the team's guest. He

Marcelo Maseda and his six-year-old daughter, Marlene, present President John F. Kennedy with gifts during his visit to Tampa in 1963. *Courtesy of Marlene Maseda Lee.*

would wear a big-league uniform and sit in the dugout while helping with batboy duties. Although concerned about his grades and his position on the Jefferson High School football team, principal D.M. Waters and coach Bill Harker urged him to attend. Marlene, who recorded many of her father's memories, wrote that the Reds considered him their good luck charm.

After the Reds were beaten by the Yankees, it was the eighteen-year-old adept Maseda who analyzed the series in a column for the *Tampa Tribune*.

The Reds repeated as NL champs in 1940 and, according to Swope, again "took up a collection among themselves and sent him [Maseda] the money so that he could come north and attend every game of the World Series with Detroit's Tigers as their guest. They not only paid his railroad fare and hotel bills, but again let him put on a uniform and see the big games from their bench. And after they won the World Series, the Reds players gave him some extra spending money to take back with him to Tampa."

Even in 1943, when World War II travel restrictions prohibited teams from training in the South, Marcelo paid his own way to the Reds' training camp one thousand miles away in Indiana. "I was so sad when I learned that the Reds would not come to Tampa this spring," Marcelo was quoted as saying in the March 18, 1943 issue of *The Sporting News*. "So, I began figuring how I could go to them wherever they trained," he said. "I finally arranged to get a leave of absence from my job for the training period, saved up my money for transportation and came up here."

His impact on the Reds was measured by Swope: "Marselo [*sic*] may or may not contribute anything of real value to the drive the Reds intend to make toward this year's pennant, but your correspondent's opinion is that he will. He typifies the spirit Bill McKechnie is striving to instill in the Reds and his zeal is of the contagious sort."

The Reds' embrace of Maseda was indicative of how they felt about their spring training home. Team officials had dismissed overtures from other cities hoping to get the Reds to relocate. The city, meanwhile, had remained patient while the Reds struggled with sub-.500 records in each of their first seven years in Tampa and no finish better than fourth place in the National League in their first eight seasons.

The Sporting News observed: "Those men who were inclined to be fickle in regard to the Reds didn't control the city's baseball committee. Those who did control the committee assumed the attitude that the Cincinnati club was making a sound start toward building a successful organization and that Tampa probably would regret it a few years hence if the Reds were invited to do their training elsewhere. So, Tampa stood by the Reds and the Reds stood by Tampa and now the fans of this city are as proud of the champs as are the fans in Cincinnati."

February 26, 1942. Reds Night at MacDill Air Force Base saw more than fifty players and staff at the Enlisted Men's Club. Sergeant Hank Greenberg, one of the Reds' rivals, was one of the masters of ceremonies. Greenberg was able to play games at Plant during the war for the MacDill Fliers while he was stationed at the air force base.

March 8, 1942. A record crowd of 4,732, including 2,207 soldiers, saw the Indians trip the Reds, 5–3. Commissioner Kenesaw Mountain Landis was present as well. After the game, many of the soldiers crowded into the nearby USO Club on South Boulevard.

March 22, 1942. The Reds' annual Latin America Day featured Miss Evelyn Fernandez, queen of the Latin Carnival, throwing out the first pitch. The crowd was 4,668, including 2,184 military men. The Dodgers' twenty-year-old right-hander, Chester Kehn, who never won a game in the big leagues, pitched six perfect innings to earn a 7–1 win.

9

WAR STORIES

In an emergency session with Commissioner Kenesaw Mountain Landis on January 5, 1943, major league owners voted to restrict spring training travel for the coming season in order to help meet the needs of the military during World War II. Teams were required to train north of the Potomac and Ohio Rivers and east of the Mississippi. Plant Field would fall under the control of the military for three years.

Reds coach Hank Gowdy, fifty-three, the first player to enlist in World War I, was soon commissioned a captain in the army and reported to Fort Benning. He was one of sixteen in the Reds organization to enter the armed services.

Eight days after the league announcement, the Reds settled on Indiana University (IU) in Bloomington as their spring bivouac. Like eleven other clubs, the Reds were going from the Grapefruit League to the Long Underwear League.

But during that three-year travel ban, there was a payoff for the Cincinnati Reds. Ted Kluszewski was a freshman at IU when the Reds arrived for training in 1944. Kluszewski was there to play football. That fall, he had helped lead Indiana to the Big Ten Championship while being named to several All-America teams. "I really wasn't interested in baseball," he was quoted as saying. "Baseball was a sideline." But he played the sport in high school and, almost to pass the time, in college.

Lenny Schwab, one of the Reds' groundskeepers, was finishing up his work on the baseball field one morning at IU when the Hoosier baseball team came out to practice. "Soon," wrote *The Sporting News*, "Kluszewski, a lefthanded hitter and thrower who stands at 6-2, 205, attracted Lenny's eye by the power of his drives."

Lenny passed what he had seen of the young freshman up the chain of command until it reached McKechnie and Giles, who immediately liked what they saw. "The boy had never played a game of college baseball," wrote *The Sporting News*, "yet McKechnie and his aides liked his actions so much they urged Giles to sign him. After deliberating with university officials, they decided to wait until after the football season to get his name on a Reds contract which included a $15,000 bonus."

Kluszewski would go on to hit 251 home runs with the Reds and another 15 at Plant Field, more than any other player. After retiring from baseball in 1961, he served as a minor league and major league coach for the Reds, including a tour on manager Sparky Anderson's staff during the reign of the Big Red Machine. In 1962, he was elected to the Reds Hall of Fame after spending more than twenty years in the organization.

On August 17, 1945, the Office of Defense Transportation lifted the travel ban. Soon, Giles was finalizing plans to return to Tampa.

Ted Kluszewski was discovered by the Reds on the campus of the University of Indiana while the team was training close to home due to World War II travel restrictions. He spent more than twenty years in a Reds uniform as a player and coach. *Courtesy of the Rhodes/ Klumpe Reds Hall of Fame Collection.*

As much as any state, big changes were coming for Florida following World War II. Pollster George Gallop asked Americans, now that the war was over, what states they would most like to move to. California and Florida ranked first and second, respectively. The "Florida Dream" was being realized like never before. Its effect on spring training was profound. Baseball was on its way back to Florida like never before.

The Sporting News summed it up this way: "For three years, the American and National Leagues fought desperately to overcome hundreds of handicaps and withstand hundreds of blows that stemmed from the war, from manpower shortages to interference from nitwits and arrant publicity seekers. Back from service into the major leagues have come several hundred ballplayers to revitalize lineups, refurbish batting orders and give to the 'Big Time' picture a dramatic favor and prismatic quality unmatched in the game's history."

All attendance records for Grapefruit League baseball were shattered in 1946 as 250,442 jammed the eleven spring parks to watch the twelve major league teams in action. The previous mark was 173,000, set in 1941. An estimated 50,000 additional fans watched intrasquad and other games between major and minor league clubs.

St. Petersburg—the only city with two teams, the Cardinals and Yankees— led the way with a total attendance of 55,036. Tampa was second at 28,478 but topped the list of average per game with 3,164. How much did Florida miss spring training? Estimates put the publicity value generated from twelve teams training in the state at $10 million.

The continued presence of the military helped. At the war's peak, more than fifteen thousand military personnel were stationed at MacDill. The Reds were only too happy to have them, as evidenced by this account in the *Tampa Tribune*: "Reds General Manager Warren Giles returned around midnight from a trip to a neighboring baseball camp and went into a downtown restaurant for a sandwich before retiring. He happened to sit next to a couple of sailors and they were bemoaning the fact that they missed the last ship-to-shore boat and had no place to spend the night. Giles immediately invited them to share his suite at the Floridan Hotel and they accepted. The next morning bright and early, Giles took a peep into the bedroom he had assigned to the sailors. They were gone. But the beds were all neatly made up and the room immaculately cleaned and a one-word note written with the burned end of a match said: 'Thanks.'"

"My own outfit in France couldn't have been more considerate than those sailors," added Giles. The following spring, the military were admitted free to all games.

There was no shortage of good postwar stories emanating from the Sunshine State. Future Hall of Famer Bob Feller conducted a free three-week camp for young prospects and players returning from the service at Tampa's Cuscadan Park in January. A total of 155 registered for the camp, of whom 66 were signed to a pro contract. When he wasn't instructing, Feller spent time on Tampa Bay in his cabin cruiser.

As camp opened, Reds pitcher Jim Prendergast and infielder Benny Zientara discovered they had been fighting in the infantry close to each other in the same battle near the end of the European war but didn't see each other until they checked in at Tampa.

When fifty-three Reds stepped on the field for their first postwar workout on February 23, it was 1,062 days since they had last set foot on Plant Field. But they weren't exactly stepping on Plant dirt. The Reds shipped a ton of Cincinnati clay to Tampa in one-hundred-pound bags to help make Plant play "more like a big league diamond than in the past."

The Reds had so many returning war veterans in camp that it was possible they could start with eight in the lineup at one time.

The Reds' first Tampa game in nearly three years, on March 10, 1946, drew a crowd of 7,290. It was the second-largest crowd to watch a baseball game in Tampa, behind the 1940 all-star exhibition game. The Reds defeated the defending World Champion Tigers despite facing a combination of 1945 AL MVP Hal Newhouser and eighteen-game winner Dizzy Trout.

With so many players, there was another new wrinkle: springtime doubleheaders. On March 17, a Sunday and St. Patrick's Day, the Reds and Cardinals made Grapefruit League history at Plant Field by playing two games. A crowd of 5,656 watched the Cardinals win the doubleheader, with both games decided by ninth-inning home runs. A week later, the Reds swept their own pair from the Indians as Plant Field welcomed 5,500 fans. In the first game, the Reds rallied to win, 7–4, after the Tribe's Bob Feller left with a 3–1 lead. In the second game, Ted Kluszewski, the rookie from Indiana University, delivered a walk-off single in the ninth after Cleveland manager Lou Boudreau intentionally walked the two hitters in front of "Klu" to set up the double play. The rookie was playing in just his third game in a Reds uniform and was already drawing comparisons to Lou Gehrig at first base, according to Whitney Martin of the Associated Press.

It was even more dramatic for the minor leagues. In 1945, there had been a total of twelve minor leagues. That number would soar to forty-three in 1946 including the Florida International League and the Tampa

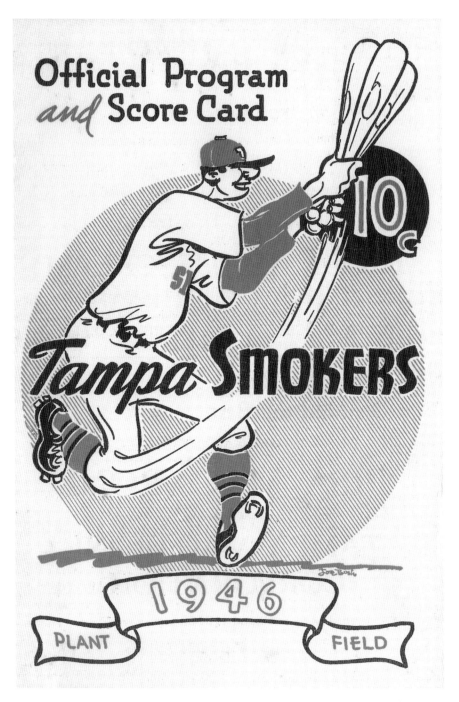

The Tampa Smokers returned in 1946 after a fifteen-year absence. *Courtesy of the Tampa Baseball Museum.*

Smokers, who were back in action after a fifteen-year, seven-month, twenty-eight-day absence.

Changes kept coming. In 1947, the First Governor's Baseball Dinner honoring executives from the teams that train in Florida was held for one hundred guests at the Floridan Hotel with Governor Millard Filmore Caldwell presiding. The following year, *Tampa Tribune* sports editor Pete Norton noticed a change in Reds camp: "Back in the olden days, if you can call 20 years or so by a dignified title, the players generally reported from 10 to 50 pounds overweight and in such terrible condition that a long, hard training grind was necessary before they were ready to play a game, and many of them never really got into condition before late May.

"Today, the slim-waisted athletes, many of them college graduates, file into hotels in quiet business suits, report for practice within a couple of pounds of their playing weight, and need little more than a week to get into game condition."

The new breed was also on top of technology. For the Reds' 1949 spring camp, Kluszewski bought an 8mm movie camera and asked his wife to film him during batting practice. The forward-thinking Reds were all for it.

MAY 30, 1942. One year before Lou Piniella was born, his father, Louis Sr., pitched four scoreless innings to earn the win as the Intersocial League All-Stars defeated the Florida West Coast League All-Stars, 9–4, before four thousand spectators at Cuscadan Park. The game benefited a navy relief fund. A U.S. Navy battalion participated in the pregame flag-raising ceremonies. That same day, Memorial Day, the United States announced it would invade Europe.

MARCH 23, 1947. Ted Williams hit a 2-run home run to lead the Red Sox to a 7–6 win over the Reds.

MARCH 15, 1948. The Reds defeated the Cardinals, 3–2, in front of 4,578 fans, including Babe Ruth, who was introduced at home plate before the game. Ruth would succumb to cancer five months later at the age of fifty-three. Hall of Famers Enos Slaughter homered and Stan Musial doubled, but the Reds won it on a walk-off double by outfielder Frank Baumholtz.

MARCH 28, 1948. The Reds defeated the Braves, 3–1, while facing Boston's two twenty-one-game winners, Warren Spahn and Johnny Sain. Ewell Blackwell threw six shutout innings, allowing only 2 hits to earn the win.

MARCH 26, 1949. Outfielder Tommy O'Brien and pitcher Jack Kramer hit the only grand slams of their major league careers to lead the Red Sox to a 10–7 win over the Reds.

April 3, 1949. Miss Clara Cuevas, Queen of the Latin America Carnival, threw out the ceremonial first pitch at the Reds' annual Latin America Day. Clara would become a beloved community figure who lived to be ninety. She attended the University of Tampa and the University of Florida and was a teacher, principal and supervisor in the Hillsborough School system. And she threw a perfect strike to Cincinnati catcher Ray Mueller.

10

MA FELDER'S

Given the segregationist nature of the South, who would have guessed that among the first future Hall of Famers to play at Plant Field, two would be Negro League stars?

The Tampa Giants of the Negro Florida State League began playing games at Plant in 1914. The following year, on September 27, they hosted the Indianapolis A.B.C. club, an independent team that would soon join the Negro League's National League. On their way to Cuba for a round of games, Indianapolis stopped in Tampa and thrashed the Giants, 12–0, while stealing 8 bases.

Their center fielder that day was Oscar Charleston, who would go on to play eighteen seasons in the Negro Major Leagues. He is considered one of the greatest all-around players in baseball history. The team's first baseman was Ben Taylor, who later compiled a .337 career average in ten seasons with five different Negro League teams. Charleston was enshrined at Cooperstown in 1976; Taylor joined him thirty years later.

Another Hall of Famer, Buck O'Neill, debuted as a professional in 1933 with the Tampa Black Smokers, who played home games at Plant Field.

It wasn't until 1950 that a Black major leaguer would play in Tampa. Over a span of three days that March, a speedy Boston Braves outfielder named Sam Jethroe became the first to play in both St. Petersburg and Tampa. In the Braves' 7–6 loss to the Reds at Plant on March 15, Jethroe went 0-for-5 before a crowd of 1,426, including some 300 Black fans, according to *The Sporting News*. There was no special mention of Jethroe in the next day's *Tampa Tribune*, which was very similar to the reaction in the *St. Petersburg Times*.

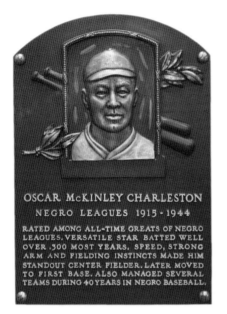 

Left: Oscar Charleston's Hall of Fame plaque. *National Baseball Hall of Fame photo*.

Right: Ben Taylor's Hall of Fame plaque. *National Baseball Hall of Fame photo*.

A veteran of the Cuban and Negro Leagues, Jethroe was thirty-three years old that spring. He went on to win the National League Rookie of the Year and led the league in stolen bases twice. He was also a favorite of Branch Rickey, who signed him for the Dodgers in 1948, but with future Hall of Famer Duke Snider in center field, Rickey sold Jethroe to the Braves for a reported sum of $100,000. "I know I am making a big mistake when I let you have this fellow," he reportedly told the Braves

While not Jackie Robinson, Jethroe had his own pressures brought about by his hefty price tag. At various times, headlines in *The Sporting News* read: "Jethroe May Be Flop in Outfield," "Jethroe Ready for Jump to Stardom?" and "Critic Finds He Lacks Jackie's Will to Win."

Harold Kaese of the *Boston Globe* seemed to concur, writing that "he cannot throw or judge a fly well enough to play center field....This Jethroe looks so fast and his arm looks so weak that it's even money he can carry the ball in from center field as fast as he can throw it in."

According to SABR's Bill Nowlin: "One might think that the signing of a black ballplayer would have been a major story in Boston at the time. It was not. Instead, the focus on Jethroe over the months through spring training was on his speed. The Boston press made little of his race."

A devout Catholic and by all accounts an affable fellow, Jethroe wore a St. Christopher medal on and off the field. "So many have been praying for me to make good. I couldn't disappoint them," he was quoted as saying.

On November 4 of that year, Jackie Robinson made his debut at Plant Park, leading his barnstorming all-star team to a 7–4 win over a Florida west coast all-star team. Dodgers Hall of Famer Roy Campanella caught the first three innings and singled home the first run of the game. Center fielder Larry Doby, also bound for Cooperstown, played the first three frames and hit a towering home run over the 385-foot fence in right field.

Robinson played the entire game at second base and singled in five plate appearances. The opposing pitcher that night was a right-hander named Walter Lee "Dirk" Gibbons, a Tampa native who, before pitching in the Negro Major Leagues for one season, grew up playing for Tampa's Pepsi Cola Juniors and Pepsi Cola Giants. According to Gibbons, after the game, Robinson was intrigued by the minarets on the top of the buildings at the University of Tampa. "I told him I would take him over there to see them and we had gone about a block before a policeman stopped us and told us we [Blacks] couldn't go any further," Gibbons told an audience at a Negro League panel discussion in 2014. "Now Jackie was a tempered man, he didn't take anything, but he told me that this was the next-to-the-last exhibition game and he didn't want to start any trouble. So, we left."

After his playing career ended, Gibbons became a supervisor at the university. "Now, I reach into my pocket," he told the audience, "and I got the keys to the whole damn campus."

Robinson and Campanella returned to Plant Field on March 20, 1952, and led the Dodgers to a 4–0 win in front of 5,028 fans, "the biggest weekday crowd to ever see the Reds in action," according to the *Tampa Tribune*. "The crowd was composed about evenly of White and Negro fans. They [Robinson and Campanella] were cheered lustily on every appearance at the plate with little partiality being noted between customers of the two races."

Writer Si Burick remembered in a piece in *The Sporting News* a long-gone sportswriter opining, not in print but in conversation, "'If Jackie Robinson plays in Tampa, there will be blood running through the gutters of our streets.'"

"There was a really good crowd at Plant Field; lots of Blacks and lots of Whites" wrote Burick. "The grandstand was always a forbidden place for Black customers; they would sit in the bleachers. On this day as the bleachers overflowed space was made available in the stands. Everybody had a wonderful time. Happily, no blood was spilled."

Robinson singled, walked, stole a base and drove in a run, and Campanella had two hits. The Dodgers were back on April 1 and, with six future Hall of Famers on the field, beat the Reds, 7–3, before a crowd of 4,552 pushing the twelve-game season total to 36,375, a new Plant Field high. Center fielder Duke Snider had 3 hits and 1 RBI, and Campanella had a double, a single and 1 RBI.

All told, Robinson played in seven Grapefruit League games in Tampa. In two of his games, attendance exceeded 7,000, a plateau that was reached only six other times at either Plant Field or Al Lopez Field in seventy springs of Grapefruit League play.

By the mid-'50s, Black players were routinely in lineups at Plant Field. Among these players were Hank Aaron, Elston Howard, Bill Bruton, Tom Alston, Vic Power, Sandy Amorós, Joe Black and Don Newcombe.

The first Black players to train in Tampa arrived in 1954. Outfielder Nino Escalera and infielder Chuck Harmon, who would become the first Blacks to play for the Redlegs in a regular season game, were in camp. (The Reds changed their name to Redlegs in 1953. Some observers believed that the political significance of "Reds" in international affairs was responsible for the change. The name was changed back for the 1959 season.) So, too, was Bill Powell, a pitcher signed from the Birmingham Black Barons the previous December who took the loss in the Redlegs' spring exhibition opener that year and thus became the first Black to wear a Cincinnati major league uniform in a game.

The White Sox, in their first year of training in Tampa with the Reds, included Minnie Miñoso on their roster. The ageless wonder had become the first African American to play for the ChiSox three years before as part of a Hall of Fame career that would span five decades.

Jim Crow laws prohibited Black players from staying with White players at the Floridan or the Tampa Terrace. "Once you leave that playing field," Reds pitcher Don Newcombe told the *Dayton Journal*'s Ritter Collett in the spring of 1960, "you step into a different world."

In *The Curt Flood Story: The Man behind the Myth*, author Stuart Weiss wrote about Flood's first night in Tampa as a rookie with the Reds in spring training in 1956. He was not only in his first camp but, as an eighteen-year-old from California, also had little experience with what he was about to encounter. "Of course," wrote Weiss, "the Redlegs hotel had no reservation for him. Indeed, the clerk turned white or, as Flood put it 'whitely' when asked the question. After recovering from his shock, the clerk looked at Flood's new suit and asked 'You with the team?' When Flood very proudly acknowledged that he was, the clerk handed him over to a Black porter who took him to a side door, waved him into a cab and told the Black driver, 'Ma Felder's.'

"The taxi deposited Flood at Ma Felder's boardinghouse almost five miles away, segregated from his White 'comrades' at the Floridan. There he lived for the duration of the Reds training camp."

Flood told Richard Carter in the book *The Way It Is* that "until it happens you literally cannot believe it. After it happens, you need time to absorb it.…Rules had been invoked and enforced. I was at Ma Felder's because white law, white custom and white sensibilities required me to remain offstage until needed. I was a good athlete…but this incidental skill did not redeem me socially."

As demeaning as it was, Flood had to admit that there was a benefit to the segregation. Wrote Carter, "Boarding at Ma Felder's, Black players had come and gone in the evenings free of the curfew that limited the hours of their white counterparts and they had seized that opportunity to drink at the local nightspots. According to [teammate] Frank Robinson some 40 odd years later his pleasure on those nights—as undoubtedly was Flood's—was limited in one vital respect. Robinson recalled he missed mixing with his white peers."

Hall of Famer Frank Robinson at Al Lopez Field. *Courtesy of the Rhodes/ Klumpe Reds Hall of Fame Collection.*

The men were there without their families. "You don't like it, but you can't fight it," Reds pitcher Brooks Lawrence, a nineteen-game winner in his first season with the Reds in 1956, told Collett. "You know it isn't the fault of the club. They do what they can. But a man would be out of his mind to bring a wife and children down here and expose them to this sort of treatment."

Black players sometimes stayed at the Pyramid Hotel on Central Avenue and also found refuge at the home of longtime Tampa physician Dr. Alfonso L. Lewis, who practiced at Clara Frye Hospital, the city's only hospital for Blacks. Players had access to the family's recreation room with a pool table, hi-fi stereo and well-stocked refrigerator.

On February 29, 1960, African American high school students, unable to get served, staged a sit-in at the lunch counter at Woolworth's in downtown Tampa, two blocks from the Reds hotel. The baseball world didn't seem to notice, but that would soon change. Spring training's civil rights issue began to be addressed publicly for the first time in St. Petersburg in the early 1960s.

The Reds' all-star outfielder Vada Pinson at Al Lopez Field. *Courtesy of Dayton Daily News Archive at Special Collections and Archives Department of Wright State University.*

The *St. Petersburg Times* believed it was no accident. "The baseball world—not its officials, but its people—recognize St. Petersburg is the hub of spring training and has decided the quickest and most efficient way to solve the problem of segregated player housing is to solve it here," wrote the *Times*.

In 1961, first baseman and future National League president Bill White began speaking up, and national sportswriter Wendell Smith began writing about it. Few other writers did, but slowly, led by the Yankees, Mets and Cardinals in St. Petersburg and Bill Veeck's White Sox in Sarasota, teams began moving to integrated hotels. It was progress, but it was obvious there was a mountain yet to move.

"We are satisfied that baseball is doing everything humanly possible to alleviate the Negro problem," said Judge Robert Cannon, legal counsel for the Major League Players Association in November 1961. "The owners have made large contributions along these lines in the last two years and we're confident they will continue to do so until all abuses have been eliminated."

In a report in the *Michigan Chronicle* on March 4, 1961, "Both the club [Reds] and hotel [The Floridan] said they never had any difficulty and were not rocking the boat." That soon changed, however. According to the *Cincinnati Enquirer*, the Reds began negotiating a new hotel deal that November. After thirty years at the Floridan, the Reds moved to the 152-room Causeway Inn Motel the following spring to accommodate all their players under one roof and allow them to share the same restaurant facilities. At least one player seemed happy with the arrangements. On the last day of camp, Vada Pinson, one of four Black players on the Reds roster, walked around with a box of autographed baseballs. "They're for the waitresses and the people who have been so nice to us here," he told the *Tampa Tribune*.

MARCH 12, 1950. Outfielder Johnny Wyrostek, who hit 58 home runs in eleven major league seasons, became the first player to hit 3 home runs at Plant Field, leading the Redlegs to a 10–6 win over the Tigers before 4,483 fans in the spring home opener.

APRIL 2, 1950. At the Redlegs' annual Latin America Day, the Braves' Warren Spahn pitched seven strong innings to defeat the home team, 7–6. Spahn left after seven innings with a 6–2 lead.

MARCH 20, 1952. The Redlegs beat the Tigers and future Hall of Famer Hal Newhouser, 1–0, in front of 5,418 fans in the spring home opener. Former Yankee Bill Bevens earned the save with three innings of 1-hit relief. Bevins had not pitched in a game against major leaguers since Game 4 of the 1947 World Series, when he was one out away from throwing the first no-hitter in

TED WILLIAMS SPIT HERE…FIRST

Five years before Ted Williams infamously spit at the fans at Fenway Park in 1956, an act that drew a $5,000 fine, he did so in Tampa at some of the 4,012 fans gathered for a game at Plant Field. From accounts in the *Boston Globe* and *Cincinnati Enquirer*, it occurred on March 18, 1951, during Boston's ugly 15–12 loss to the Reds.

"The trouble started," wrote the *Globe*'s Hy Hurwitz, "when Ted rolled out to pitcher Ken Rafensberger in the third inning and merely jogged to first base. There was no chance for him to beat the throw but the packed grandstand gave him a rough vocal going over. He turned toward the customers and spat elaborately."

Williams got his revenge in his next turn at bat, when he drilled a long home run over the 390-foot sign in right-center field. "I remember the booing," recalled Williams to the *Tampa Tribune*'s Tom McEwen in 1970. "So I hit one out of the park like it was a pea and spat at the fans."

The *Enquirer* wrote that he "expectorated" at hecklers again later in the game after striking out twice during Boston's seven-run seventh inning. Both Ks came against a rather unremarkable right-hander named Eddie Erautt. "After waving weakly for the second time at Erautt's curve for this strike," described the *Enquirer*, "Williams waved his bat around his head, as though he was going to toss it into the crowded stands, and then trotted off to the clubhouse after expectorating several times in the direction of his many hecklers."

"It was the first public spitting incident, I'm sure of that," Williams confirmed to McEwen.

The "Splendid Splinter" was apparently miffed about making the trip from Sarasota to Tampa, telling writers before the game, "Don't know why I came up here today. I have a lousy cold and just a short while ago one of those jerk sportswriters from our town asked me if the arm injury I suffered in the All-Star Game last summer would affect my throwing. Guess he didn't know that it was my left arm that I hurt and I throw with my right."

series history, but he allowed a walk-off, 2-run double to pinch-hitter Cookie Lavagetto and lost, 3–2. Bevens developed arm trouble following the series and, after repeated attempts, never made it back to the big leagues.

MARCH 22, 1952. Mickey Mantle made his Plant Field debut with 3 hits, 2 doubles and 1 RBI in the Yankees' 11–8 win over the Redlegs before 3,776 fans.

MARCH 29, 1953. Stan Musial had a home run, 2 singles and 3 RBI, and fellow future Hall of Famer Enos Slaughter added a home run and a single to lead the Cardinals past the Redlegs, 9–5.

MARCH 30, 1953. Five-foot, six-inch right-hander Bobby Shantz, the reigning American League MVP, threw a complete game in besting the Redlegs, 4–3, in their spring finale.

MARCH 26, 1954. Legendary actor Jimmy Stewart was at Plant Field to film scenes for his upcoming movie *Strategic Air Command*. Fans were use as extras in scenes filmed before that day's game between the Reds and Cardinals.

11

A TOUGH OUT

I n the official bio on the City of Tampa's website for Curtis Hixon, the city's thirty-fourth mayor whose death came during his fourth term, there is no mention of baseball. Yet it was Hixon who undoubtedly did more to keep the national pastime alive in Tampa than any of the city's other fifty-eight mayors.

At the time of Hixon's death in 1956, the *Tampa Tribune* wrote, "The mayor put the value of sports to the area ahead of many things which drew criticism from some quarters, but he never quit fighting for what he thought was best for the city and never gave up on his idea of a big sports center where he built the baseball park, Al Lopez Field."

In 1949, Hixon saw an opportunity to purchase a 720-acre parcel of land for $70,400 to build a sports complex that would include a golf course, tennis courts, a football stadium and a spring training ballpark.

After twice failing to get the Tampa Board of Representatives to approve, Hixon remained what baseball scouts would call a "tough out" and secured the vote.

As bids were about to be solicited, Hixon's mettle was to be tested again. This time, it was the start of the Korean War, which made Hixon's project a casualty. "I don't want to start work on anything I cannot finish," the mayor was quoted as saying in the August 9, 1950 edition of the *Tribune*. "Right now, it appears to me that the unsettled state of world affairs makes it unwise to start work on a project that would require a considerable amount of steel, the most vital product in war preparedness."

Mayor Curtis Hixon (*center*). *Courtesy of Tampa-Hillsborough County Public Library System.*

It wouldn't be until January 9, 1953, that the idea was revived and the bid process restarted on a five-thousand-seat, $400,000 park to be located at the entrance to Drew Field Airport, a U.S. Army Air Force base that later became Tampa International Airport.

Hixon's challenges weren't over. The next hurdle came on July 31, when the cheapest of three bids for the construction came in at $590,000, almost $200,000 higher than expected. As a result, the mayor agreed to delay the building of the ballpark for a year. Wrote the *Tribune*: "In his recommendations that all three of the bids be rejected, Mayor Hixon said the city did not have money to be spent in such large amounts for the baseball stadium. City officials indicated that the bid process would begin again in approximately three months with no strict date set for completion."

In the meantime, Hixon was determined to bring a second major league team to Tampa. He wanted what St. Petersburg had. One of the big factors in favor of the new stadium was the possibility of luring another club. "I've been thinking along these lines for some time," Hixon confidently told the *Tampa Tribune*. "I think it would be the proper thing to do for the clubs since Tampa is the hub of spring training in Florida." Hixon had his sights set on the Chicago White Sox, who had trained in Winter Haven in the spring of 1924. The Sox were a logical target, having bounced around eight different cities in four states since then.

The Sox were led by their visionary, quotable general manager, Frank Lane, who also happened to be a winter resident of the Tampa Bay area. The White Sox had several other reasons for wanting to leave their latest post in El Centro, California. With more teams, Florida offered Chicago more opportunities for games against major league competition. And teams in California needed to wrap up spring training early to accommodate the Pacific Coast League schedule. Not so in Florida.

Just as spring training in 1953 finished, Lane agreed to bring the Sox to Tampa with the understanding that the new ballpark would be ready by the 1954 spring season.

When the news landed that the inflated construction bids would delay the completion date for the stadium, Lane nonetheless remained committed to Tampa and Hixon for the 1954 spring season. The Sox would share Plant Field with the Reds for their games while city crews worked on building a proper practice field on the proposed stadium site that would be ready for the new tenants by mid-February. Temporary bleachers would be erected to allow spectators to watch the White Sox during their workouts. They were also promised a "temporary shanty on the premises for bathhouse and clubhouse purposes."

Tampa would become only the third Florida city to host two spring teams, joining St. Petersburg and Jacksonville, and the White Sox would become the sixth team to train in Tampa.

The Sox began workouts on February 21, and the Reds started four days later after city workers removed a large platform left over from the Florida State Fair from the Plant Field infield.

The March 6 spring opener between the Reds and White Sox was rained out. The next day, the White Sox prevailed, 8–3, before 2,514 fans. Ferris Fain, the White Sox two-time AL batting champion, had 3 hits, and Bill Fischer earned the win. Fischer would be back in Tampa Bay nearly fifty years later as the pitching coach of the Devil Rays.

With the two teams playing a combined nineteen games, thirteen future Hall of Famers and a dozen or so bright young African American stars came through Tampa that spring. And the first nationally televised

---

PLANT'S FINAL BLOOM

Although no one was quite certain at the time, the Reds-Yankees game on March 29, 1954, was the last major league game played at Plant Field. The Redlegs would practice at Plant from 1955 to 1959 and again in 1961 and 1962, but the spring of 1955 would be Plant's first without a game, aside from the World War II travel ban years (1943–45), since 1918.

The final pitch was thrown by Yankees ace Allie Reynolds, and it was hit over the fence near the center field scoreboard by Ted Kluszewski for a ninth-inning, two-run home run, giving Cincy a 9–8 walk-off win. It was Kluszewski's 15th career home run at Plant, more than any other player.

Dodgers versus White Sox on March 28, 1954, one of the final games played at Plant Field. *Courtesy of Tampa-Hillsborough County Public Library System.*

Grapefruit League game took place at Plant Field on March 13, when the Tigers thumped the Redlegs, 9–5. But overall, the results of the two-team format were disappointing. One-quarter of the team's combined attendance was generated from one game, which saw the White Sox host Jackie Robinson and the Dodgers. The two teams drew less than 1,000 fans in eleven of the other eighteen games. Across the bay, the Cardinals and Yankees—buoyed by a tourist season that welcomed more than 44,000 visitors to St. Petersburg—drew 91,825 fans for twenty-five dates, an average of 3,673, nearly two and a half times Tampa's average of 1,508.

It wasn't altogether surprising. *The Sporting News* wrote before the start of camp, "Whether the experiment will be as much of a financial success as it has been in St. Pete seems doubtful, because Tampa is not a tourist town with hosts of idle visitors looking for some way to pass the time."

Less than a month after the two teams left to go home, on April 20, Hixon announced that the contracts for the new ballpark were complete and that construction would begin soon. The construction firm J.S. Stephens had submitted the winning bid at $255,451. Thanks to Hixon's perseverance, Tampa was indeed finally getting a new baseball stadium. It would be located between Himes Avenue and Dale Mabry Highway, on the north side of Tampa Bay Boulevard.

But while the city got its new ballpark, it lost its beloved Smokers on the evening of May 5 due to its "weak financial situation." Ironically, the second baseman on that club was Mike Ilitch, who would go on to create Little Caesar's Pizza and own the Detroit Tigers and the National Hockey League's Red Wings. At one point, his worth was estimated to be $6.1 billion.

Two months after Tampa's ballpark announcement, the City of Clearwater said it, too, would have a new ballpark in 1955. Jack Russell Stadium would be the Grapefruit League home of the Phillies.

12

A MONUMENT TO A
"MAN WITHOUT AN ENEMY"

At the official field dedication of Tampa's new ballpark on March 20, 1955, the commissioner of baseball, Ford Frick, was there. Also present were the president of the American League, Will Harridge; the top brass and players from the park's two inhabitants, the Redlegs and White Sox; Indians general manager and soon-to-be-Hall of Famer Hank Greenberg; Tampa mayor Curtis Hixon; and 3,325 fans.

Not present was the ballpark's namesake: Alfonso Ramon Lopez.

As manager of the Cleveland Indians, Lopez was busy with a ballgame of his own in the Cactus League some 2,500 miles away. He had, however, seen Al Lopez Field, albeit unfinished, the previous October on Al Lopez Day, when Mayor Hixon officially named the park and presented him with the keys to the 8,600-seat stadium that featured a design similar to that of Miami Stadium. It was a symmetrical park with measurements of 342 feet down the foul lines, 377 to the alleys and 400 feet to center.

Meanwhile, the event on March 20 was more about the community and less about the man. And that, no doubt, was exactly what "El Señor" preferred. *The Sporting News* wrote the following: "The dedication was more than the ceremonial opening of another ballpark. It was a personal tribute to a former player not only because he has risen to distinction in his profession, but because he has won a special place in the affection of those who know him best—the folks of his native city. In this there should be food for thought for everyone in baseball.

Construction of the grandstands at Al Lopez Field. *Courtesy of Tampa-Hillsborough County Public Library System.*

"His long career as a catcher, his success as a manager in the minors and his eventual advance to authority in the majors undoubtedly were factors in his selection for this Tampa tribute. But behind the flowing compliments paid him March 20, is the story of a man without an enemy, a man who remained as simple, as humble, as thoughtful of his fellow citizens when he became nationally famous as when he was a struggling youngster in Ybor City. Perhaps there is no other city in the country where a big-league manager occupies the identical place in his hometown that Al Lopez enjoys in Tampa."

Commissioner Frick spoke that day in accord. "I want to take this opportunity to congratulate Tampa on having produced such a fine gentleman as Lopez and also on having built this jewel of a ballpark."

The son of Spanish immigrants, Lopez became the first Tampa native to play in the majors. He grew up on the sandlots of Ybor City and at Plant Field, but baseball equipment in the household was a luxury. As a youngster, he broke his nose during a game because he didn't have a catcher's mask.

When reminiscing about his youth, Lopez stated: "I think that we enjoyed our boyhood an awful lot. You could go not too far from where you were and you could build up your own baseball diamond. We used to build our own, put the bases down, and make our own baseball diamond in any couple of open fields that we had."

"I didn't have a chance to finish my high school career," remembered Lopez to *The Sporting News*. "I attended Sacred Heart [later known as Tampa Jesuit], a Catholic boys school for one year, but after the tenth grade I never

Al Lopez and Mayor Curtis Hixon at a Tampa parade celebrating Al's Indians winning the 1954 AL pennant and the impending christening of Al Lopez Field. *Tampa Tribune photo.*

went to school again. It was during my one year at Sacred Heart [who played its home games at Plant Field] that the idea came into my mind to make professional baseball a career. Coach Frank McKenna was the man who directed all sports at the school and told me that I had enough talent to make a living in baseball.

"At that time, I had no choice about quitting school. We needed the money at home and it was either take some other kind of job or go into baseball as a pro." According to the Tampa Baseball Museum, Lopez was already "delivering Cuban bread for a Ybor City bakery for a few dollars a month."

His father, Modesto, was a tobacco worker who died before seeing his son make it to the big leagues. Al's mother, Faustina, wanted her son to be a sheet-metal worker.

He signed with the Florida State League's Tampa Smokers in 1925 at the age of sixteen for $150 a month. Referring to the "Horseshoe" on Franklin Street, *Tampa Tribune* columnist Tom Ewen wrote, "Al was signed to a Tampa Smokers catching contract on a pool room cigar counter."

That same spring, he was hired by the Tampa-based Washington Senators to catch batting practice during spring workouts at Plant Field. Years later, Manager Bucky Harris confirmed to *The Sporting News* that Lopez was paid $2.50 per day to catch.

"Occasionally I would work out with the team," Lopez told *The Sporting News*. "Muddy Ruel and Benny Tate were the regular Senators catchers and they helped me considerably by showing me the finer points of the catching business."

That offseason, Lopez caught the legendary Walter Johnson in an exhibition game in Ybor City. Author Wes Singletary described the experience this way: "Before the game began, Johnson took the understandably nervous Lopez aside and instructed him not to call for too many curve balls. Lopez responded, 'Mr. Johnson, you throw whatever you want to; I'll put down the sign and if you don't want it then shake it off.' Johnson advised Lopez that he would only let it all out against a couple of hitters that had traditionally given him trouble. After the contest, Johnson told a listener, 'That boy did real well back there; handled himself fine.'"

The Sporting News quoted Lopez as saying, "After the game he patted me on the head and said 'Someday you're gonna make a great catcher,' boy, I'll never forget it." At sixteen, Lopez was deemed by the Senators to be too young to sign.

His career in professional baseball would span forty-four years. He caught more than 1,900 games and managed another 1,400. In 1945, Lopez surpassed Gabby Hartnett's major league record for career games as a catcher, a mark that was not broken until 1987. In 1977, he was elected to the National Baseball Hall of Fame.

Dizzy Dean once called him "undoubtedly the greatest fielding catcher and the best receiver in baseball history."

In the offseason, Lopez couldn't wait to be home with his family and lifelong pals. "There's never a day when I'm in Tampa when some of my cronies fail to drop by the house and talk baseball," he told the *Tribune's* Pete Norton. Dominoes or a game of hearts at the Latin social clubs were almost always a part of his daily offseason routine.

Another future Hall of Fame manager was witness to that scene. "Dad would take me to the Cuban Club in the offseason and I'd watch him play dominoes with Al. It was very important to me," Tony LaRussa told Tom McEwen of the *Tribune*.

So, in the spring of 1955, while Lopez was piloting the Indians out West, play began at Al Lopez Field. The White Sox first christened the field with

Rookie Tony LaRussa and Al Lopez in 1963. *Courtesy of Tampa Baseball Museum.*

their early workouts, while the Redlegs trained at Plant Field before moving over to Al Lopez Field to play their games. It was at Plant Field on March 1 that Cincinnati startled the fashion market when they debuted their iconic vest uniform tops over a brilliant-red, long-sleeved shirt.

Also new at Al Lopez that spring were three future Hall of Famers who were wearing a major league uniform for the first time. The Reds' nineteen-year-old outfielder, Frank Robinson, and the White Sox's twenty-one-year-old infielder, Luis Aparicio, would call Al Lopez Field home. It would be another year before either would play in a regular season game. And there was the Pirates' twenty-year-old outfielder, Roberto Clemente, who hit a home run at Lopez Field as a visitor on March 21, his first in a major league uniform, two weeks after Frank Robinson did the same thing.

In the opening game of the new park on March 10, a Thursday afternoon, the Redlegs committed 8 errors, and it was a Hall of Famer who hit the first home run in the White Sox's 10–7 win before 3,025. Minnie Miñoso's fourth-inning grand slam won him a Gibson Market Master freezer-refrigerator, courtesy of Florida Frozen Food Products of Tampa.

On March 27, it was the Dodgers and their Hall of Fame contingent of Jackie Robinson, Duke Snider, Roy Campanella, Pee Wee Reese and Gil Hodges that drew the largest home crowd of the season. The White Sox edged Brooklyn, 4–3, in eleven innings before 5,052, spoiling a spectacular Sunday afternoon for Robinson, who went 4-for-4 and stole home on the front end of a triple steal. Hodges went 3-for-3, but Miñoso doubled and scored the winning run, walk-off style. (The following season, the Dodgers would break their own Lopez Field attendance record when 7,500 fans [6,957 paid] showed up to see Brooklyn beat Chicago, 4–3, in eleven innings on April 1. The park was bursting at the seams, including a section in the bleachers down the third-base line for "colored" fans. Each team walked away with an unheard-of sum of $4,000 as their share of the gate receipts.)

Two major things occurred the following spring involving the White Sox. On March 10, 1956, in the spring opener, a Sox 4–3 victory over the Reds, five-foot, seven-inch shortstop Luis Aparicio and five-foot, eight-inch second baseman Nellie Fox turned their first double play together. The smallest keystone combination in the majors, the two future Hall of Famers would go on to play alongside each other for seven years, starting 1,015 regular season games together. They also played together in six World Series games, three All-Star Games and dozens of other Grapefruit League games. Two weeks later, on March 22, in his first Grapefruit League season, recently acquired Larry Doby, a former Negro League all-star and future Hall of Famer, hit 2 home runs and drove in 5 to lead the White Sox to an 8–6 win over the Braves.

Six months later, on the last weekend of the regular season, came more news that would impact the White Sox. Al Lopez announced his resignation as manager of the Indians after what he described as "six trying years." While the Tribe won the AL pennant in 1954, they finished second to the Yankees in the five other years.

As soon as they were made aware, the Indian players, perhaps thinking Al was retiring, called a meeting. According to *The Sporting News*, "A few minutes later, Lopez was invited into the session. 'Al,' said ace Bob Feller, 'we hate to see you go. We've enjoyed being with you for the past six years and for putting up with us we want you to accept this little gift.'" They had collected $400 with which to purchase new golfing gear. It was reported that several players were teary-eyed.

If it was retirement, it lasted exactly thirty days. On October 29, the White Sox announced that Lopez would be their choice as manager to replace Marty Marion, who had resigned a week earlier. Lopez was forty-eight years old and still had the fire that was behind Bob Lemon's quote about his former manager: "The hardest thing about losing is to look at Lopez' face."

The *Chicago Tribune*'s Jerome Holtzman shared more than a few meals with Lopez. "He worked so hard and was so wound up in the game that most times after a loss he couldn't eat solid food, so he'd have soup for dinner."

His hiring meant that it would be the first time Lopez would enjoy being home for spring training. It would also put him in a class all by himself, managing in a venue bearing his name.

For the first time, professional baseball would be played all summer long at the two-year-old park, as Tampa returned to the Florida State League, this time as the Tarpons. They celebrated the first league championship on Al Lopez Field that summer when they defeated Palatka, 3–2, on September 4. And in 1958, baseball would be played there ten months a year with the advent of the Florida Instructional League. With a three-month schedule, the league was designed to accelerate the growth of the game's best prospects.

Also causing a stir was the weather and some experimental rules put in place by Major League Baseball for the spring. Lopez took some ribbing about the rain and cool weather that limited workouts. "I haven't been in Florida at this time of the year since 1940 [when he was in camp with the Braves in Bradenton]," Lopez responded to critics, "but people tell me this is the worst weather for late February early March in 30 years."

The rules drawing the most attention were those involving the twenty-second pitch clock and the prohibition of batters stepping out of the batter's box once the pitcher is ready. Lopez was concerned about the latter rule, which he believed would increase the number of "quick pitches" thrown. "It's gonna get someone killed," complained El Señor.

Overall, Lopez was enjoying his extra time in his hometown. The 1957 spring opener on March 9 was preceded by a parade of both the White Sox and Reds, joined by three hundred Little Leaguers who were guests of both teams at the game. Temperatures in the low fifties and twenty-mile-per-hour winds kept many fans at home. Cincinnati made it worse for Al by beating the Sox, 8–4, but his troops went 6-3 in their first season there.

While Chicago finished with ninety wins for the 1957 regular season, an improvement of five games, it was another second-place finish for Lopez, his sixth in seven years of managing.

MARCH 17, 1957. The Yankees beat the Reds, 9–0, before 6,932, the largest crowd to see the Reds play in Tampa. The switch-hitting Mickey Mantle celebrated St. Patrick's Day with 2 home runs, one from each side of the plate.

MARCH 21, 1957. The Braves' Johnny Logan and Wes Covington each hit 3 home runs to lead the Braves to a 10–7 win over the White Sox. In major league history, only once have teammates hit 3 home runs in the same regular season game: Richie Sexson and Jeromy Burnitz did it for the Brewers in a game in 2001.

MARCH 27, 1957. The Braves' Joe Adcock hit 2 home runs, including a grand slam, and Hank Aaron added another as the Braves beat Cincinnati, 12–6. Warren Spahn worked seven innings and allowed 2 runs to get the win.

APRIL 2, 1957. Stan Musial went 5-for-5 with 4 singles, 1 home run and 4 RBI as St. Louis defeated the Reds, 9–2.

FEBRUARY 1958. Always on the cutting edge, Redlegs general manager Gabe Paul introduced air-conditioned caps in spring training. The caps featured a water-cooled band made of aluminum foil and insulite sponges with a perforated vinyl cover inserted into the cap. The idea was quickly abandoned.

MARCH 18, 1958. The Senators beat Chicago, 10–0, as twenty-one-year-old Ralph Lumenti (who won exactly one game in his major league career) beat thirty-eight-year-old Early Wynn (who won exactly three hundred games). Lumenti allowed 4 hits in six innings.

MARCH 22, 1958. The Phillies edged the White Sox, 6–5, in sixteen innings at Al Lopez Field on a balk by pitcher Gerry Staley. The Sox loaded the bases in the bottom of the inning on 3 walks, but Future Hall of Fame center fielder Richie Ashburn ended the game when he caught Billy Goodman's fly ball and nailed Earl Battey at the plate in a game-ending double play. Robin Roberts, also bound for Cooperstown, pitched six shutout innings, allowing just 2 hits. Another Hall of Famer, Chisox second baseman Nellie Fox, played all sixteen innings.

13

A BIG WIN, A BIGGER LOSS

The 1959 baseball season ended in pure joy for all Tampa baseball fans. Their favorite son, Al Lopez, finally caught the Yankees: Lopez's "Go-Go" White Sox took the American League pennant, the only season in a ten-year span that New York failed to win it. In doing so, Lopez became the first White Sox manager to win a pennant in four decades.

New Tampa mayor Julian Lane was sworn in on October 1, and his first official act as mayor was to send a telegram to Al wishing him luck that afternoon against the Dodgers in Game 1 of the World Series.

On the night of September 22, following the White Sox's pennant-clinching win at Cleveland, there was "rejoicing, dancing in the streets and citizens embracing each other with happy cries of 'Viva Lopez,'" according to *The Sporting News*.

Three weeks later, the reception awaiting Al and his wife, Connie, when they stepped off their Eastern Airlines flight at Tampa Municipal Airport was just as festive. No one cared that the Sox bowed to the Dodgers in the World Series. A big sign with "Welcome Home Al" in big red letters greeted them, and the Ybor Elementary School Cojunto Ybor, a rumba band, played. The next day, after a quick trip to the dentist to care for an infected tooth, Lopez and his family were part of a twenty-five-car motorcade that paraded in Ybor City, wound through Tampa and culminated at Al Lopez Field for more ceremony.

It was far different than the way the baseball season had begun that year. At the Thirteenth Annual Governor's Dinner in March at the Tampa

Al Lopez returned home to find a huge celebration waiting for him at Tampa Municipal Airport in honor of the 1959 White Sox AL Championship season. *Tampa Tribune photo*.

Terrace Hotel, Governor LeRoy Collins stated that he believed Tampa fans and businessmen had failed to give adequate support to the Reds and White Sox. "We can't take this fine thing that we have [big league clubs training in Florida cities] for granted," the *Tampa Tribune* quoted him as saying.

"Clubs have been training in Tampa for many years, but we hear rumors that teams now here may be forced to move because of the lack of patronage.

I also feel that attendance at these Grapefruit League games is a problem not only for Tampa, but for all of the state of Florida. Certainly, we want these big leaguers to know we want them, appreciate them, and appreciate what they have done in the development of Florida." The governor continued by asking civic groups to get behind a ticket push.

"We can't sit idly by, and do nothing," he continued. "I can see no reason why teams training in Florida, whether in Tampa or anywhere else in the state, cannot play to packed stands."

There was immediate pushback. Wrote the *Tribune*'s columnist Ralph Warner, "They [Reds and White Sox] are fully within their rights to ask chamber men for help in increasing attendance. Chamber folks are supposed to rally around such causes. It is doubtful though, if club chiefs will make progress by hinting they may move from the city if more fans don't turn out. Ideally located, offering the best in facilities, a variety of the finest dining places and good accommodations. Tampa is the hub of the spring training belt. Tampa isn't going to be without spring baseball."

National writers like Dan Daniel of *The Sporting News* clapped back with a warning. "Florida apparently believes it 'has it made.' It hopes that in time all 16 clubs will be based there. But the state would do well to come out of its complacency and eliminate the feeling that the 12 clubs are captives. Florida is taking the ball teams for granted. That's a dangerous philosophy…the state and the various cities in which the big leaguers are based should show more active interest in what they are getting and what could develop from these benefices."

Coincidentally, a shining example of such a development emerged just as spring training was closing. On March 31, August A. Busch Jr., president of the Cardinals and the Anheuser-Busch Brewery, was presiding over the dedication of Busch Gardens, a $500,000 landscaped park on the site of his company's new brewery in the city's Temple Terrace section.

At the dedication, Busch commented that it was visits with his ballclub in St. Petersburg that acquainted him with the Tampa Bay country and the people from this area. This firsthand knowledge and his fondness for the businesspeople he met brought Busch to the decision to erect a multimillion-dollar brewery in Tampa, one of only four cities with an Anheuser-Busch plant at the time.

Tensions were rising, and rumors were circulating that Tampa was about to lose one of its teams. The stories got more intense just as spring camps opened when news broke that the imaginative maverick Bill Veeck was buying controlling interest in the White Sox from the feuding Comiskey

Aerial view of
Busch Gardens at
its opening in 1959.
*Courtesy of Tampa-
Hillsborough County
Public Library System.*

family. The *Tribune* quoted an unnamed inside source as saying: "It's a messy situation and funny things could happen. It certainly is untimely. Here's a team ready to start spring training and the players and other personnel don't know who'll they will be working for."

Lopez said he didn't believe the situation would bother the players at all, but one anonymously told the *Tribune*: "Sure, I'm worried about it. Veeck is known as a free dealer. I worry about being traded and so do some of the other players. I've picked up second place money with Chicago. I would hate to be traded to a lower club." During the first week of camp, a judge cleared the way for the sale. Two weeks later, Veeck was in Tampa circulating among the baseball folks.

Cincinnati players showed up at camp with questions of their own when they found former Notre Dame University football coach Terry Brennan in a Reds uniform. Brennan, who had coached 1956 Heisman Trophy winner Paul Hornung three years earlier, was in camp at Plant Field to oversee the Redlegs' conditioning program. "I have given this serious consideration for many years," said Reds general manager Gabe Paul. "Some years ago, we tried to get Paul Brown [Cleveland Browns cofounder and head coach] to do the job for us, but he declined at the last minute. The reason we wanted a name coach wasn't the publicity angle, but for acceptance of the idea by the players themselves."

Even more of a radical departure from the usual spring training policy was the addition of Lucky McDaniel to Reds camp. McDaniel was a target-shooting expert who believed he could sharpen the batting eyes of

Gus Bell practicing at Plant Field with the minarets of the Tampa Bay Hotel in the background. *Courtesy of the Rhodes/Klumpe Reds Hall of Fame Collection.*

ballplayers by teaching them air rifle marksmanship. McDaniel wasn't back the following spring, but he made an impression; Gabe Paul encouraged the players go to a skeet-shooting range near Tampa airport.

The biggest story of camps all around the state was none of these. It was what remains to this day the worst March weather in Tampa's history, with a record 12.64 inches of rain. Given the governor's comments and the need to increase spring attendance, it couldn't have come at a worse time.

By spring's end in 1959, the Grapefruit League had suffered twenty-nine rainouts, while the Cactus League had but one while averaging 3,003 per game to Florida's 2,024. It represented a 40 percent increase for those four teams training out West, while the twelve teams in Florida collectively fell .08 percent. A millionaire Arizona rancher made an offer to send a new tarpaulin to each of the Florida teams. In their early workouts at Plant Field that spring, Reds pitchers were forced to throw in a cow barn normally reserved for the state fair.

It got so bad that, in the middle of a week of rained-out games, the resourceful Paul called his Dodgers counterpart, Buzzie Bavasi, and suggested that both teams fly to Cuba for a brief series.

Bavasi agreed. After having their flight delayed a day by the weather, the Reds arrived in Cuba from Tampa on Friday, March 30, and the two teams played a weekend series that drew a total of 11,055 Cubans for the two games. The highlight of the trip may have been the players' accommodations at the beautiful oceanfront Havana Hilton.

On the field, things were just as strange. At the Lopez Field spring opener on March 7, the Reds' budding star center fielder, Vada Pinson, belted a ninth-inning walk-off grand slam, breaking a 3–3 tie with the White Sox. Pinson, however, passed the base runner in front of him, Elio Chacón, between first and second base and had to settle for a walk-off single. After the game, according to *The Sporting News*, Cincinnati third-base coach Reggie Otero told Pinson, "You must remember that Chacón is a rookie."

"I know," protested Pinson, "but I'm a rookie, too."

Two days later, White Sox third baseman Billy Goodman made 3 errors, but it wasn't a game-high. Pittsburgh first baseman Dick Stuart committed 4, including 3 in one inning. On April 1, Chicago pitcher Ray Moore hit a home run in an 8–5 win over the Braves. It broke a streak of thirteen homerless games for the light-hitting Sox. For the entire spring, Chicago hit only 5 home runs at Lopez Field, matching the same number Frank Robinson hit there for the Reds.

That same spring, the Reds and White Sox played Tampa's first Grapefruit League night game as part of a Fan Appreciation celebration. The two teams agreed to play under the Lopez Field lights, which were not up to major league standards. According to the *Tampa Tribune*, "The game was arranged to see just how well Tampa would support spring training baseball if given a better chance." There were approximately 3,500 fans in the park that evening, including 2,464 paid admissions. They saw an exciting game that ended on White Sox center fielder Jim Landis's walk-off home run.

In the spring finale on April 5, the Reds beat the Yankees, sans Mickey Mantle, in front of 5,017 fans. But the season-high crowd wasn't enough to change the White Sox opinion of Tampa as a future spring home. Two days later, they announced that beginning in 1960, they would train at Sarasota's Payne Park, a site abandoned by the Red Sox a year earlier.

The numbers were not pretty. In twelve games at Al Lopez Field, the Sox drew 13,792 fans, lowest among the sixteen major league clubs. Conversely, in nine road games, Chicago attracted 21,737. Their six-year run in Tampa was over. "We hate to leave and we're not mad at anybody," said the Sox's embattled young vice-president, Chuck Comiskey, to the *Tribune*. "If we just could have drawn a few more people to our games, I don't think the move ever would have come about. We certainly don't expect anybody to pay for our spring training. We know it will cost us money. But we simply don't want it to cost as much as it has. In Sarasota, we hope the books will balance out a little better."

The following spring, the reigning American League champion White Sox broke the Sarasota attendance record by drawing 37,744, shattering the previous mark of 32,330 set by the 1956 Red Sox.

According to Bob Addie in the *Washington Post*, Lopez was asked if he was going to try to take Al Lopez Field with him to Sarasota. Al replied, "I wish I could, that's a beautiful field."

MARCH 14, 1959. Non-roster rookie right-hander Bob Gibson earned what would have been a five-inning save (saves didn't become an official statistic for another ten years) in the Cardinals' 12–6 win over the White Sox. The Cards scored 6 runs in the first inning and 6 in the second, all against Sox starter Dick Donovan.

APRIL 24, 1959. The biggest crowd to see a Florida State League game in Tampa, 8,851 fans, came out to see the Tarpons split a doubleheader with the Palatka Redlegs. Free tickets were distributed to customers by the Winn-Dixie Kwik-Chek grocery chain. Palatka's Vic Davalillo, who would play sixteen seasons in the big leagues as an outfielder but who pitched in the minors, got the loss in the first game and the win in the nightcap.

FEBRUARY, 27, 1960. With the White Sox off to Sarasota, the Reds begin spring training workouts at Al Lopez Field. Excluding the three years when there was no Florida spring training due to World War II travel restrictions, it was the first spring Plant Field did not host major league players. Cincinnati's Southern Association team, Nashville, began working out at Plant on March 11, and three other Reds farm clubs held workouts there at various dates through the first week of April. The Reds did return to Plant for workouts during the first couple of weeks of spring training in 1961 and 1962.

MARCH 20, 1960. With 5,762 in attendance, the biggest for a Reds game since 1957, the Yankees ripped Cincinnati, 13–5. Yogi Berra hit a 3-run home run, and Roger Maris singled 3 times to lead Casey Stengel's troops.

APRIL 3, 1960. The Reds' Vada Pinson homered off the defending World Champion Dodgers' top starter, Don Drysdale, in an eight-inning, rain-shortened game that ended 4–4. The third rain shower of the day halted the game for good. Despite the weather, 4,645 fans showed up, bringing the final total to 22,971 for nine games.

MARCH 26, 1961. In a World Series preview, the Yankees beat the Reds before 6,596 fans on a Sunday afternoon. It was the second-largest crowd to

Al Lopez Field hosted two championship teams in 1961: the Reds won the NL pennant, and the Tarpons won the Florida State League title. *Courtesy of the Rhodes/Klumpe Reds Hall of Fame Collection.*

see the Reds at Al Lopez Field. Mickey Mantle had 3 strikeouts, equaling the number of times he had fanned all spring.

APRIL 4, 1961. Frank Robinson hit his 5th home run of the spring at Al Lopez Field as the Reds closed out the home schedule with a 6–5 win over the Phillies. Rookie Dwight Siebler balked in the winning run in the bottom of the ninth. Reds pinch-hitter Jerry Lynch had tripled to start the inning.

MARCH 24, 1962. Sandy Koufax won his Al Lopez Field debut, 7–4, in front of 2,784 fans. Koufax pitched seven innings and allowed only 1 earned run.

MARCH 25, 1962. Roger Maris hit 2 home runs to lead the Yankees past the Reds, 6–3, in front of 4,863 waterlogged fans.

APRIL 24, 1962. Team captain Tony LaRussa hit a 3-run home run at Cuscadan Park in the City High School championship game in a 13–0 win over Chamberlain. Less than two months later, on June 20, at Al Lopez Field in his third pro game, he went 3-for-3 with 3 RBIs and a stolen base to lead the Daytona Beach Islanders, the Athletics' affiliate in the Florida State League, to a 10–9 win over the Tarpons.

14

A JOYFUL BEGINNING, A TRAGIC END

While the Reds were engaged in a scoreless struggle with the White Sox under threatening skies in their 1963 spring home opener, a young non-roster rookie not scheduled to play in the game was taking some extra swings on one of four new practice diamonds adjacent to Al Lopez Field. For the first time in their thirty springs in Tampa, Reds minor league players and the major leaguers were training together.

The rookie wasn't on the game roster that day, and as he left the practice field thinking his day was over, one of the Reds coaches, Dave Ryba, said to the young prospect, "Stick around kid, the way this game is going, anything is liable to happen."

With the game scoreless in the ninth, Cincinnati manager Fred Hutchinson put the rookie in as a pinch-runner, and he remained in the game as the third baseman. On his first trip to the plate in a Reds major league uniform, he doubled in the eleventh inning but was stranded. He came to the plate in the fourteenth and doubled again. The next batter lifted a routine fly ball to the outfield, and the rookie tagged up and rushed to third ahead of the throw from the startled outfielder. One batter later, he scored on a single through the left side of the infield, giving the Reds a 1–0 win, snapping their season-opening twenty-two-inning scoreless streak.

Thus began the major league career of Pete Rose.

"That [game] got me in the big leagues," Rose told the *Tampa Tribune* years later. According to Earl Lawson in the August 17, 1963 edition of *The Sporting News*, it was that "precocious dash that earned him the nickname

Rookie Pete Rose at Al Lopez Field in 1963. *Courtesy of the Rhodes/Klumpe Reds Hall of Fame Collection.*

'Charlie Hustle.'" Soon after, Yankees Mickey Mantle and Whitey Ford stuck him with the name after his aggressive baserunning against the Yankees in a spring game.

Two years before, he was known as "Scooter" while winning the 1961 Florida State League Player of the Year award as a member of the champion Tarpons. On August 13 at Al Lopez Field, he became the first FSL player to hit 30 triples in a season and added 2 more in the postseason.

In 1984, *Tampa Tribune* columnist Tom McEwen asked Rose what he remembered about that season in the FSL. "Triples," he told McEwen. "I sure remember those triples here. Tony Curry had the record for triples with 12. After a month and a half, I had 13."

Rose returned that fall as a member of the Reds' Florida Instructional League team. Years later, George Kissell, the longtime baseball guru of the St. Louis Cardinals, told Glenn Miller of the *St. Petersburg Evening Independent* that he remembered seeing Rose in the FIL that fall. "He was a second baseman and he came by third base one day. He said 'I'm gonna make the Hall of Fame.' I said, 'How you gonna do that?' He said, 'I'm gonna get 200 hits a year for ten years.'"

And that is exactly what he did.

According to the *Tampa Tribune*, Hutchinson said of Rose, "The kid is as hard as this," while pounding the iron supports of the batting cage at

Clearwater during a conversation with Phillies manager Gene Mauch before a game later that spring. Dave Bristol, Rose's manager at Macon in 1962, said, "A scout clocked him at 4.1 [seconds] going to first base on a walk and that's faster than most guys can run. We heard a Cleveland scout clocked him at 4.3 here in the winter league, he must have been tired that day."

Rose, of course, was never tired. It didn't matter if it was a regular season game or an exhibition contest. He felt a responsibility to excel for himself and the fans.

In his book *The Main Spark*, Hall of Fame manager Sparky Anderson described Rose's actions during a game with the Reds Triple A affiliate Indianapolis. "I told Pete he would bat once; then he could go to the clubhouse and get dressed. But he made an out his first time up and asked to stay in. Next time he lined a single. I knew when he took off he wasn't going to stop at first. He rounded the bag and kept going. About two-thirds of the way toward second base, he took off and made it safe to the bag with a giant belly-whopper, his spectacular type of diving slide.

"Pete got up, brushed himself off and waited for the pinch runner to come in for him, then ran off the field to the tune of thunderous applause. Back on the bench he grinned and said, 'That's what these people came for, Sparky.'"

Playing second base against the Dodgers at Al Lopez Field on March 31 of his first major league camp, the brash Rose even decoyed veteran Maury Wills, perhaps the best base runner in the majors coming off a 104–stolen base season. Wills was on first base when Dodgers third baseman Ken McMullen hit a drive single to left field. Rose noticed that Willis didn't pick up the ball and shouted, "I've got it," from his second base position, sending Wills back toward first. He barely made it to second.

"They say I'm cocky," Rose told the *Tampa Tribune* his first year in major league camp. "Well, I believe you've got to be cocky to get anywhere. I'll do anything they tell me to do to get to the major leagues."

The Reds were confident in Rose as well. Midway through the 1963 season, they traded popular second baseman Don Blasingame to Washington to free up the spot for the twenty-two-year-old.

The spring ended on a positive note as the Reds drew a total of 28,757, the team's high since moving to Al Lopez Field. It was bolstered by the largest paid crowd in Al Lopez Field history, the 8,359 who turned out to see the Reds beat the Yankees on St. Patrick's Day in a game televised back to both markets. Reds left fielder Wally Post homered and doubled, and Rose added a pair of singles. Mickey Mantle homered in a losing cause.

The park's new electronic scoreboard was functioning for the first time, but not without incident. A blackout hit the city of Tampa at 10:15 a.m. and returned at 1:29 p.m., one minute before first pitch.

There was, however, a bigger crowd yet to come at Al Lopez that year. The Orioles and Reds were scheduled to play a Florida Instructional League game on November 18, but it was moved to Clearwater to accommodate a special visitor. Future Hall of Famer and Big Red Machine member Tony Perez didn't mind; he singled and doubled that day at Jack Russell Stadium.

No one else minded, either. John F. Kennedy was in Tampa for only half a day, but for a few minutes he would be at Al Lopez Field, speaking to a crowd that filled all of the park's 9,400 seats and had some spectators sitting on the roof of the Reds' new minor league offices. They had been there since 10:00 a.m. awaiting the 1:35 p.m. presidential visit, the first made to Tampa by a sitting chief executive. It would be the president's only public appearance on the stop. While most of the FIL players were off to Clearwater for the game, their families stayed behind to hear what Kennedy had to say.

President John F. Kennedy meets Roland Manteiga, owner and editor of Tampa's *LaGaceta* newspaper, at Al Lopez Field. *Courtesy of* LaGaceta.

President John F. Kennedy speaks to an overflow crowd at Al Lopez Field on November 18, 1963, four days before he was assassinated. *John F. Kennedy Presidential Library and Museum photo.*

Cincinnati Reds business manager Al Stevens "pondered the crowd wondering if JFK wouldn't sign as a shortstop for the club," reported the *Tampa Tribune.*

"On that sunny day Nov. 18, 1963," wrote the *St. Petersburg Times* thirty years later, "Tampa was positively giddy with optimism, thrilled to share the spotlight with the charismatic young president. On that day, the president could step out of the pocket of security and spontaneously connect with people. Children were forgiven if they skipped school to see him."

It was all part of an observance of the fiftieth anniversary of commercial aviation, specifically Tony Jannus's historic flight from St. Petersburg to Tampa, the world's first scheduled commercial airline flight, which took place on January 1, 1914. During his nine-minute speech, Kennedy praised Jannus's "foresight, pioneering spirit and fortitude," all of which, he said, helped explain why the United States "leads the world in all endeavors." He also showed empathy to some four thousand cigar factory workers whose jobs were lost due to the trade embargo he activated against Cuba some twenty-two months before.

And then he was off the platform, smiling graciously and shaking the hands of many of those along the Al Lopez Field fence line. As his motorcade made off for his next stop, at the Fort Homer Hesterly Armory, it passed near the Dale Mabry Drive-In Theatre, where the movie *The Great Escape*, starring Steve McQueen, was playing.

Other than the dusting the president's green-and-white marine helicopter gave to those with infield seats at the ballpark on its arrival, it was indeed a well-executed escape. And while the local Ku Klux Klansmen made it known they didn't embrace the country's first Catholic president, 415 of Tampa's police officers maintained the peace on an unforgettable, historic afternoon filled with promise.

Oddly, the next day, the regularly scheduled FIL game was played, and on the same spot where the president spoke, a rookie infielder for the Washington Senators named John Kennedy delivered a 2-run single in the Nats' game against the Athletics. Stranger still, the two Kennedys shared the same May 29 birthday.

It was perfect. And then, of course, it wasn't. Almost exactly seventy-two hours after JFK exited Al Lopez Field, he was killed by a sniper's bullet. "Tampans," wrote the *Tampa Tribune*, "appeared to feel the shock of the crime all the more vividly because of the president's recent trip. In that four-hour visit he had become a live, personal friend to thousands."

Three of the four FIL games were stopped midgame on hearing of the president's death, including the Reds' 3–0, five-inning win over the Cardinals at Lopez Field. All games were canceled the following day

---

"He Threw Me Out of My Own Ballpark"

On April 2, 1963, Al Lopez was in the visiting dugout at Al Lopez Field, managing the White Sox, who by then had moved their spring training camp from Tampa to Sarasota. Lopez vigorously disputed an interference call against Sox pitcher Joel Horlen, who was covering first base on a ground ball hit by opposing pitcher Jim O'Toole. Lopez was ejected by umpire John Stevens, unofficially becoming the first to be removed from a game in a ballpark bearing his name.

Recalled Lopez to the *St. Petersburg Times*, "He [Stevens] said, 'One more word out of you and you're gone.' I said, 'You can't throw me out of this ballpark. This is my ballpark, Al Lopez Field.' He said, 'Get out of here.' He threw me out of my own ballpark." The Sox fell, 7–0, to the Reds that Tuesday afternoon.

BENCH'S QUICK BAPTISM

On June 8, 1965, the Reds selected catcher Johnny Bench from Binger (Oklahoma) High School in the second round of the June draft. After signing two weeks later, he was on a plane to Tampa. His flight from an Oklahoma airport touched down at Tampa Airport at 8:57 p.m., and within the hour he had caught the ninth inning of the Florida State League Tampa Tarpons' 3–0 win over Coco Beach at Al Lopez Field.

"I'll never forget it," Bench said to the *Tampa Tribune* years later. "I was just 18 years old and I got off the plane. A pitcher on the disabled list picked me up and took me to the ballpark. Naturally, you just don't sit down. They put you in a uniform. I went down to the bullpen and warmed up a pitcher and then I was in the game."

and, like almost every other event nationwide, on the day of the funeral. A baseball fan, JFK had thrown out the first pitch at three season openers.

On December 10, the Tampa City Council voted unanimously to change the name of Grand Central Avenue to John F. Kennedy Boulevard, where two weeks before thousands of people had lined miles of that roadway to get a glimpse of the president. A few months later, Rose, too, was honored when he received his 1963 National League Rookie of the Year award on Opening Day at the ballpark just a couple of miles off Kennedy Boulevard.

MARCH 25, 1964. Phillies rookie Richie Allen hit 2 home runs, giving him 6 in the spring, as the Phillies beat the Reds, 7–1, before a Ladies Day crowd of 1,003.

MARCH 29, 1964. Mickey Mantle hit a pair of home runs off Joe Nuxhall to lead the Yankees past the Reds, 6–4. Mantle's blasts were opposite-field to right and right-center. The game was televised back to New York on WPIX with Mel Allen, Phil Rizzuto and Jerry Coleman calling the action.

MARCH 14, 1965. Pete Rose's 2-run home run in the eighth provided the winning

Johnny Bench in the spring of 1968. *Courtesy of the Rhodes/Klumpe Reds Hall of Fame Collection.*

margin in Cincinnati's 5–4 win over the White Sox in the spring home opener. The crowd of 4,240 was the Reds' best for a home opener in thirteen years.

MARCH 28, 1965. Frank Robinson's 3-run, first-inning homer off Yankees starter and future best-selling author Jim Bouton powered the Reds to a 4–2 win before a Sunday afternoon crowd of 7,357 at Al Lopez Field.

MARCH 30, 1965. In the afternoon, Frank Robinson hit a home run to help lead the host Reds past the Minnesota Twins, 7–3, and in the evening, Frank won the annual Major League Baseball Bowling Tournament at Tampa's East Gate Lanes. Robinson defeated Washington first baseman Roy Sievers, 212–145, in the finals.

APRIL 7, 1965. Cincinnati closed out the spring with a 5–3 win over the Twins and the Grapefruit League title. Two future Hall of Famers, reigning AL batting campion Tony Oliva and Reds rookie third baseman Tony Perez, homered at Al Lopez Field, as did Pete Rose.

MARCH 24, 1966. Rookie Don Sutton worked five innings and allowed 1 hit in leading the World Champion Dodgers to a 6–0 win over the Reds. Half of the Dodgers' switch-hitting infield led the attack: shortstop Maury Wills had 3 singles and scored 2 runs, and first baseman Wes Parker added 2 doubles.

MARCH 26, 1966. More than six hundred people attended the Twentieth Annual Governor's Dinner at the Sheraton-Tampa Motor Inn. St. Louis sportscaster Jack Buck emceed the festivities, attended by representatives of the sixteen Florida-based major league clubs and seventy-nine minor league teams. That afternoon at Al Lopez Field, Phillies rookie Grant Jackson and

AL LOPEZ FIELD: THE PLACE TO BE SEEN

Senators prospects Dick Bosman and Don Loun combined to throw a no-hitter against the Florida Instructional League Reds on November 23, 1965. Nats manager Gil Hodges was one of the few people in the stands that day. "It was a turning point for me," recalled Bosman, who had spent that season at the Senators' double A affiliate. "I begged them to send me to instructional league because in those days you knew you were going to be seen." After catching Hodges's eye, Bosman received a non-roster invite to big league camp the next spring and, later that season, was pitching in the major leagues. In 1969, he led the AL in earned run average.

veteran Dallas Green, who would go on to manage the Yankees, Mets and Phillies as well as serve as general manager of the Cubs, combined to shut out the Reds, 5–0, with Bob Uecker behind the plate.

March 28, 1966. The "Atlanta" Braves played their first game at Al Lopez Field, and the Reds prevailed, 5–2, as Milt Pappas, acquired from Baltimore in the offseason for Frank Robinson, earned the win. Pappas worked five innings and allowed only 2 hits and 1 run. Phil Niekro started for the Braves and allowed 1 run in three innings.

April 5, 1966. In the spring finale, the White Sox outlasted the Reds, 2–1, in seventeen innings. Gene Freese's single scored pitcher Bruce Howard with the winning run. Howard worked five scoreless innings to earn the win. Pete Rose played all seventeen innings.

15

BUCS FEVER

As much as Tampa was proud of its decades-long relationship with the Reds, there was something it wanted more. The National Football League had entered its expansion era. Tampa wanted in.

On the same day as the Reds' first workout of spring training in 1966, the city council voted five to two in favor of constructing a fifty-two-thousand-seat, $4.6 million football stadium to get the NFL's attention. It was to be built on the 720-acre tract the city had purchased as a potential sports complex in 1949, adjacent to Lopez Field. While the baseball field would remain, the team's cluster of practice fields would have to be moved.

The heavy machinery of the Jones-Mahoney construction company began dismantling the team's minor league complex, including its four fields, clubhouse and offices, just four months before the start of the 1967 Grapefruit League season. Never mind that the complex was not even five years old or that the Reds had not yet renewed their agreement with the city to return. Football was on the mind of all Tampanians.

All was not lost. The city donated land to the stadium overseer, the Tampa Sports Authority (TSA), to build a cloverleaf of fields for the Reds minor leaguers a few blocks south of Lopez Field at Himes Avenue and Columbus Drive. No one, however, had figured out who would pay for the approximately $60,000 in construction costs.

In mid-November, after several weeks of posturing, the Reds, the TSA, the Tampa Chamber of Commerce and the city settled their differences. The fields would be ready by spring, and the administration/clubhouse building would come sometime later.

As it turned out, the fields initially were somewhat less than industry standard. The infields were soft, and the outfield grass died due to a severe winter drought season. According to *The Sporting News*, "The Reds contended that left fielder Pere Rose and second baseman Tommy Helms suffered pulled muscles running in the soft sand in the early days of spring training when the squad was so big that Manager Dave Bristol divided it between Al Lopez and the farm camp."

In the ensuing summer of 1967, a summer romance evolved when the City of Tempe, Arizona, approached the Reds after learning of their displeasure with Tampa. Tempe offered to build a $3 million complex to entice the Reds to leave Tampa after thirty-four years.

But on September 8, the summer love faded as the Reds and their new president and general manager, Bob Howsam, announced they would return extending Major League Baseball's longest spring training partnership. "Tampa Not Tempe, Gets Reds," noted the *Tampa Tribune* cheerily.

While the minor league clubhouse and offices wouldn't be ready by spring (they were being designed as a recreation center when not in use), the city's

Al Lopez Field (*foreground*) and Tampa Stadium. *Courtesy of Skip Gandy Commercial and Aerial Photography.*

With Tampa Stadium in the background, minor league manager Don Zimmer (*center*) and Reds manager Dave Bristol (*right*) were among those supervising the workouts at Al Lopez Field in 1967. *Courtesy of the Rhodes/Klumpe Reds Hall of Fame Collection.*

chamber of commerce budgeted $150,000 in improvements and additions and another $5,000 to the major league clubhouse at Al Lopez Field. Permanent batting cages, an observation tower, restrooms, reconditioned fields, sprinkler systems and center-field backdrops would be ready for the spring of 1968. It wasn't until the spring of 1969 that the entire project was completed, but it was worth the wait. "Absolutely first class, a credit to all involved," lauded the *Tribune*.

Tampa got their football venue and kept its longtime major league tenant. And the Reds got something else, too: a new form of conditioning. Training in the shadow of a fifty-thousand-seat stadium wasn't lost on the organization's farm director, Chief Bender, and minor league managers Don Zimmer and Sparky Anderson. Reds farmhands were required to run up and down the stadium steps every day, two trips of one hundred stairs the first day and three trips thereafter.

The only negative came when the University of Tennessee pounded the University of Tampa, 38–0, in the first game at Tampa Stadium (aka the Big Sombrero) on November 4, 1967, in front of twenty-seven thousand fans.

And on April 24, 1974, the Tampa Bay Buccaneers were welcomed into the National Football League.

March 26, 1967. Two months before announcing his retirement, Whitey Ford earned a win over the Reds, 9–3, before 5,590 on a Sunday afternoon at Al Lopez Field. Ford scattered 9 hits and 3 runs over five and two-thirds innings. He would win only two more games.

March 23, 1968. Twenty-one-year-old Reggie Jackson hit a home run in a morning "B" game to lead the Athletics past the Reds, 2–1, at Al Lopez Field. Jackson went 0-for-3 in the regular game that afternoon on Helmet Day for kids. It would be the last game in Tampa for the Athletics, who had first visited in 1914. They would train in Arizona in 1969.

March 28, 1968. Tigers starter Denny McLain, about to embark on a thirty-one-win season, pitched six innings, allowing only 1 hit, a home run to Vada Pinson, but he was likely on his way back to Lakeland when the Reds won, 4–3, in fourteen innings on third baseman Don Wert's throwing error. Willie Horton homered for the Tigers.

April 3–4, 1968. Thirty-six-year-old Jim Bunning threw a complete game, scattering 10 hits to lead his new team, the Pirates, to a 4–3 win over the Reds in the Al Lopez Field spring finale. The Reds broke camp the next day hours before the news broke that Dr. Martin Luther King had been assassinated in Memphis. The following day, the Reds announced they would postpone their season opener scheduled for the following Monday, April 8. Eventually, all openers were pushed back forty-eight hours.

June 18, 1968. By a vote of six to two, the Tampa City Council approved the sale of beer at Al Lopez Field.

March 15, 1969. Harry Carey and Jack Buck broadcast the game on KMOX radio from the box seats directly behind home plate at Al Lopez Field as the Cardinals edged the Reds, 3–2. Johnny Bench homered in a losing cause.

March 25, 1969. The host Reds beat the defending World Champion Tigers, 16–1. Tony Perez collected 2 doubles, 2 home runs, 4 runs scored and 6 RBI.

April 2, 1969. In Atlanta's 10–0 win over the Reds, Satchel Paige, listed as an assistant trainer with the Braves, was on hand at Al Lopez Field. One day later, the bespectacled sixty-two-year-old Paige earned a win against the Braves' International League affiliate, Richmond, in Savannah, Georgia.

December 9, 1969. High winds and driving rain forced a DC-3 cargo plane to land in the parking lot of Al Lopez Field. No one was injured. One wing rested ten feet from the fence surrounding the field.

March 12, 1970. Tampa native and reigning AL Rookie of the Year Lou Piniella made his first appearance at Al Lopez Field as a major leaguer. His

---

THE COMEBACK

On March 27, 1969, against a stiff wind blowing in from left field at Al Lopez Field, Boston's Tony Conigliaro hit a home run. As Will McDonough from the *Boston Globe* pointed out, it had been 603 days since his last one. Conigliaro missed all of 1968 after being hit in the eye by a pitch from the Angels' Jack Hamilton on August 18, 1967. Reds manager Dave Bristol was among those cheering on Conigliaro. "I don't like to see anybody hit home runs against us, but in his case, it's a little different." Conigliaro went on to hit 20 home runs that season and a career-high 36 the following year before his eyesight deteriorated, ending his career.

---

parents, aunts, uncles and cousins were all there as Lou got the Kansas City Royals' first hit of the game in the fifth inning of a 3–0 loss to the Reds. It was his first visit there since 1963, when he played center field for the Senators' Instructional League team.

MARCH 15, 1970. Pete Rose's headfirst slide into home in the bottom of the ninth inning capped the Reds' 3-run rally as they beat the Mets, 7–6, in front of 4,076 on a Sunday afternoon. Nolan Ryan made his Lopez Field debut and worked four innings, allowing only 1 run, and World Series hero Jerry Koosman worked the first four innings.

MARCH 10, 1971. Chamberlain High School graduate Steve Garvey played in his first major league spring training game at Al Lopez and contributed a double and 2 singles in the Dodgers' 13–2 win.

MARCH 14, 1971. A crowd of 8,492, the largest to see the Reds play in Tampa, saw a combination of players from the Phillies, Cardinals and Mets win, 4–2. Having an odd number of teams training in Florida (seventeen) made some makeshift combination teams necessary. Frisch's Restaurants provided free tickets to the game. Simultaneously, the American Gold Cup Horse competition was being held inside Tampa Stadium. The two events drew more than 20,000 on a warm Sunday afternoon.

MARCH 26, 1971. Johnny Bench, playing with ten stitches in his lower right leg from a spike wound suffered only days before, hit 2 home runs to lead the Reds to a 10–5 win over Boston.

16

THE BIG RED MACHINE

When Dave Concepción walked out on the fields of "Redsland," the team's practice facility near AL Lopez Field, on a balmy Thursday spring morning, history of sorts was made. The Reds' twenty-three-year-old Venezuelan shortstop-in-waiting was a couple of days late joining his teammates in Tampa. The date was March 2, 1972.

His presence meant that the primary working parts of Cincinnati's Big Red Machine were in place together for the first time. They were Concepción, Johnny Bench, Tony Perez, Pete Rose, George Foster, Ken Griffey Sr., Joe Morgan and Cesar Geronimo, the latter two having been acquired as part of an eight-player trade with Houston the previous November. The pack would become known as the "Great Eight."

Morgan, as Griffey referred to him in his book *Big Red: Baseball, Fatherhood and My Life in the Big Red Machine*, was "the final bolt in the Big Red Machine."

This group (except Griffey, who didn't debut until 1973) would be together for the next five seasons, during which the Reds would win ninety-five or more games each season and advance to the postseason four times, including three World Series appearances. *Sports Illustrated*'s Tim Crothers listed the Big Red Machine as the seventh most dominant team in sports history.

Years later, Anderson told Joe Henderson of the *Tampa Tribune* that the beginnings of the Reds' incredible run could be traced to 1970, his first year with the club. "Nobody has ever written this about that ballclub but that's the only club I've ever heard of that that broke camp in Tampa with eight pure rookies. People just want to remember the Big Red Machine, but that didn't happen overnight. The Machine started with that team."

In 1975, Tampa celebrated the Reds' first of two consecutive world championships. *Tampa Tribune photo.*

The following year, Anderson began tinkering under the hood of the machine just weeks after the Reds had closed out 1971 with a three-game losing streak, clinching a very disappointing sub-.500 season.

Anderson and General Manager Bob Howsam sent an unheard-of eight major leaguers to their Florida Instructional League team in Tampa for the winter. Included were Foster and Concepción and, for ten days, Bench. The FIL had been known to aid individual player comebacks. Maybe in the Reds' case, it could revive a team.

The 1972 Big Red Machine was even going to get a fresh coat of paint. A few days after Concepción arrived, on March 9, the Reds introduced their new double-knit, pullover-style uniforms made of stretchy synthetic material. Bench, Rose, pitcher Don Gullet and University of South Florida cheerleader Gail Carroll modeled the new look for the media.

Spring training was going to change, too. "No player is going to swing the bat before noon," Anderson told *The Sporting News.* "Until then, we'll work on a lot of things that cost us so many games this [past] season. It may get so monotonous to the players. They'll be 'This is ridiculous, we've been doing this for years.' But I don't care if they've been doing the same thing for thirty years. I'm tired of guys blundering in June and then saying 'I'm sorry, it was my fault.'"

One of Sparky's most important adjustments came in that first spring of 1970. While Bench had been used exclusively behind the plate during his first three seasons in the big leagues, Anderson had an idea to increase his plate appearances and reduce the wear and tear of catching on his young bull. "I am convinced this guy can play anything except second base and shortstop," said Anderson as his first camp at the helm began. "If he can play 25 or 30 games somewhere else besides catching, then he gets a rest from catching and someone else rests."

In an intrasquad game at Al Lopez Field on March 4, Bench played the entire game at third base for the first time. He went on that season to win the first of two National League Most Valuable Player awards while starting 130 games behind the plate and another 22 at other positions, including 2 in centerfield. Bench would go on to play at least three positions for the next eight seasons and, over the ensuing six seasons (1970–75), averaged 650 plate appearances per season. No other catcher averaged 600 during that span.

While 31,750 fans attended Reds games in 1971, just the second time the team eclipsed the 30,000 mark in its thirty-eight-year history in Tampa, the spring was marred by contract holdouts and injuries that likely led to their season-killing 20-32 start.

In the spring of 1972, there was another set of challenges, including an eight-game losing streak, a disastrous three-game trip to Venezuela during which they scored just 1 run in losing all three games to the World Champion Pirates and the threat of a work stoppage, which, in fact, occurred when the players walked out the final week of the spring season, a delay that lasted fourteen days.

The Venezuelan trip, arranged as a goodwill gesture by the commissioner's office, didn't go well off the field, either. Both teams were plagued by continuing travel delays, prompting one player to tell the *Tampa Tribune*, "If I ever have to make the trip again, I'm going to come up with a bad leg excuse."

There was also the matter of the Reds' spring training home schedule, called by the *Tampa Tribune* the "shortest and poorest in years." It included only ten games, two of which were lost by the labor situation. It did not include one Saturday date or any games at all with the Yankees, Red Sox or Orioles. Reds management promised to do better.

On March 31, Cincinnati blasted the Royals, 10–1, before 6,890 fans who were there—despite a morning tornado warning—courtesy of Frisch's

Restaurants. Tony Perez hit 2 home runs. A few hours later, the players voted to strike. Two days after the players left camp, the Reds moved their operation back to Cincinnati. Rose and pitcher Gary Nolan continued their own workouts in Tampa.

Challenges aside, the Reds went on a 26-6 run in May and June, secured first place in the NL West for good on June 25 and finished 10.5 games ahead of the second-place Astros. It ended with a World Series loss to Dick Williams's Oakland A's.

Tampa fans responded the following spring, as 31,550 flocked to the thirteen home games on the improved 1973 schedule.

It was more of the same in the spring of 1974 after the Reds won the 1973 NL West with ninety-nine wins. The team drew an average of 2,738 fans per game, a 13 percent increase from the year before per game, despite the nation's fuel crisis, which limited travel.

Anderson called it the Reds' best version of the Big Red Machine. "It's the best spring we've had. We have had the best weather, the best working club and this is the best team we've had," he told the media just before the club flew north for Opening Day. The Reds won 98 games, good enough to win any division that season except their own, thanks to the Dodgers' 102-win season.

Before the Reds' 1975 spring camp opened, Pete Rose opened a restaurant, Johnny Bench got married and Sparky Anderson pumped the brakes slightly on the Big Red Machine. "Every year you feel like you have a good chance to win, but last year there was no doubt about it," Anderson told the *Tampa Tribune* in February. "I think I got them overconfident. We're going to stop talking about winning and world championships. We just need to do our work and other things will take care of themselves."

Meanwhile, fans from all over Tampa Bay were excited. It started in Bradenton on Opening Day, which drew 4,463 spectators, a record for the fifty-three-year-old McKechnie Field. At Al Lopez Field, the Reds drew 4,000 or more six times and shattered the season mark by drawing 46,232 for fourteen dates. There was definitely something in the air. The Reds beat the Mets and Tom Seaver on March 17 and the Yankees and Catfish Hunter on March 27 and, in a World Series preview, outlasted the Red Sox in a memorable 1–0 win in sixteen innings on April 4. None of Boston's eight position players came out of the game—all Red Sox regulars, including future Hall of Famers Jim Rice and thirty-five-year-old Carl Yastrzemski. Two female streakers made an appearance in the eleventh inning. Almost as embarrassing were the Red Sox hitters, who were 4-for-49.

Among those rooting on the Reds was eight-year-old Tino Martinez. "The Reds were our team," recalled Martinez, one of the most celebrated major leaguers to come out of Tampa. "We loved the Reds. A highlight for us was maybe two times a spring we would leave school early, my dad would pick us up and we would go see the Reds play at Al Lopez. I vividly remember them playing the Dodgers and seeing [Chamberlain High School grad] Steve Garvey and getting autographs from him and Don Sutton.

"Some of the players, Johnny Bench and Dave Concepción for sure, would come by my dad's cigar factory to get cigars and we would have the chance to meet them and get our picture taken with them. Like every other kid I wanted to be a ballplayer."

Also in the stands, was 2023 Hall of Fame inductee Fred McGriff, who lived in Lincoln Gardens, a community located close to Al Lopez Field. In his induction speech at Cooperstown, McGriff told the crowd of approximately ten thousand, "I lived less than a mile from where the Reds played and from time to time me and my friends got tickets to the games, the Big Red

Tino Martinez (*right*) with brothers Tony (*center*) and Rene Jr. (*left*) and Reds Hall of Famer Johnny Bench at Al Lopez Field circa 1975. *Courtesy of the Martinez family.*

Tony Perez participating in spring conditioning drills at Al Lopez Field. *Courtesy of the Rhodes/Klumpe Reds Hall of Fame Collection.*

Machine. The best part about those games was that if you got a foul ball and returned it to the team you got a Coke and a hot dog. We couldn't wait for a foul ball and the mad scramble to begin."

Infielder Tom Foley, who would go on to play thirteen major league seasons, including his first three with the Reds, remembers having a locker on what the players called "rookie row" at Al Lopez. "Bernie Stowe was the clubhouse guy and he was the one who would come and get you off the field when you were getting cut. I remember him walking down our row of lockers holding an imaginary hand grenade. He pretended to pull the pin with his teeth and roll it down the aisle to our lockers. It was funny, most of us knew it was gonna happen eventually on rookie row.

"I also remember once Bernie came on the field during batting practice and headed for one of the outfielders. The guy saw Bernie and dropped his glove and ran, jumped over the fence at Al Lopez and kept going. They got him though."

After a slow start in the regular season, the Reds went 88-34 after May 20, clinched the 1975 NL West crown with three weeks left in the season and won four 1-run games out of seven over the Red Sox to win Cincinnati's first World Championship since 1940.

Three months before, the first-year expansion Tampa Bay Rowdies won the North American Soccer League championship at Tampa Stadium. It was

"Champa Bay I," with the sequel coming some forty years later, when the NHL's Lightning and NFL's Buccaneers both won World Championships.

Tampa mayor William Poe sent the following telegram hours after the Reds became champions: "300,000 citizens of the City of Tampa send their warmest congratulations to you for being World Champions. We know there is a little Tampa clay on your cleats."

Who would have guessed that when they returned in the spring of 1976, the Reds couldn't even find a place to practice? With baseball's reserve clause at the center of the discord, major league owners activated a lockout at all spring camps on March 1. A number of Reds showed up at Redsland but were denied access. The group, led by Johnny Bench, unsuccessfully appealed to the University of South Florida for use of the school's ballfield. "It was a matter of policy," stated USF athletic director Dick Bowers, who told the *Tampa Tribune* that over two hundred requests from the community had already been turned down.

The group wound up practicing at historic Macfarlane Park in West Tampa. Twenty-some Reds players and one of Tampa's favorite sons, Lou Piniella, now a Yankee who had played on the same field as an eleven-year-old, were taking part in the unsupervised workouts when the Mets' Tom Seaver, one of the more active player representatives, suggested halting the informal gatherings. By working out, Seaver reasoned, the players were helping the owners and weakening their own bargaining position.

Players on most of the teams followed that suggestion. Reds players did not. "I'm proud of them," Reds general manager Bob Howsam told *The Sporting News*. It was Howsam's way of praising the players for making up their own minds, not being a flock of sheep.

Meanwhile, the minor league camp opened at Redsland, and the organization didn't miss the opportunity to sell Reds 1975 champion beach towels, key rings, posters, ashtrays, pillows, pennants and more.

Finally, without a settlement, Commissioner Bowie Kuhn ordered the owners to open the camps on March 17, and the Reds began formal workouts the next day at 10:00 a.m. with twenty-three players present. Bench hit the first batting-practice home run of the morning off former Reds pitcher-turned-broadcaster Joe Nuxhall. The Reds canceled eight home games at Al Lopez Field and hosted the Houston Astros in their spring home opener on March 28, one of five home games they would play. There were 5,727 in the stands, the first 5,000 of whom got a color team photo of the 1975 World Champions. Present among the group were the resilient 570 members of the Reds Rooters fan club on their annual pilgrimage from Cincinnati. They

Reds manager Sparky Anderson and Dave Concepción at the batting cage during spring training workouts at Redsland. *Courtesy of the Rhodes/Klumpe Reds Hall of Fame Collection.*

saw the Astros and big right-hander J.R. Richard clip the Reds, 9–6. All-star center fielder Cesar Cedeno had 4 hits for Houston.

The mood picked up a little more that day when the Reds announced that shortstop Dave Concepción had arrived from Venezuela and signed his contract.

But the rest of camp was not as positive. After twenty days, the Reds left for Cincinnati on April 6 following a lackluster, hastily played thirteen-game spring schedule. Reds pitchers allowed 7 or more runs in nearly half of those games. "I think when you have a set club, basically the guys are just trying to get into shape," Anderson rationalized as the Reds broke camp. "Some are busting it, but mentally on the whole there is no enthusiasm in spring training.

"I am real pleased with the condition of our players. I know years ago the Yankees used to fiddle around in the spring and play about .500 ball while Washington won everything and you can't do that in the spring. To win you've got to grind it out during the year."

And grind they did. The Reds took over first place for good in the NL West on May 29 and then swept through the postseason without losing a game to the Phillies or Yankees to become the first National League team since the 1921–22 New York Giants to win back-to-back World Series Championships.

As Cincinnati celebrated, the Mets' prospects beat the Reds, 9–2, in a Florida Instructional League game. The beat went on at Al Lopez Field.

MARCH 11, 1973. The spring home opener drew 5,820 fans on a warm, sunny Sunday afternoon as the Reds fell to the Tigers, 13–8. Lieutenant Colonel Richard Keirn threw out the ceremonial first pitch to Johnny Bench. Keirn, a Tampa native, had recently returned home after seven and a half years as a prisoner in Vietnam.

MARCH 28, 1973. Willie Mays made his Al Lopez Field debut and lined a run-scoring double in three trips, and Tom Seaver pitched six innings of 2-hit ball as the Mets shut out Cincinnati, 8–0.

MAY 13, 1975. Mark "The Bird" Fydrich made his Al Lopez Field debut for the Florida State League's Lakeland Tigers. Fydrich was one out from a complete-game 2–1 win when the Tarpons' Dean Graumann hit a ground ball that took a bad bounce over the head of shortstop Melvin Jackson, scoring 2 runs for a 3–2 Tampa walk-off win.

MARCH 30, 1976. Mike Schmidt hit his first Al Lopez Field home run in the Phillies' 7–1 win. Ken Griffey Sr. accounted for the Reds' only run with an inside-the-park home run.

Pete Rose and Tony Perez at Al Lopez Field. *Courtesy of the Rhodes/Klumpe Reds Hall of Fame Collection.*

17

A SPRING OF DISCONTENT

A l Lopez was playing gin rummy at Palma Ceia Country Club on a chilly January afternoon when he got the news: That summer, he would be among the National Baseball Hall of Fame's class of 1977. El Señor spent the rest of the day receiving calls and visitors at his home on Tampa Bay as the city celebrated its first Hall of Famer. It turned out to be the only good baseball news in Tampa that spring.

The *Tribune* called it "a spring of discontent…amid contract gripes, walkouts and fistfights." There was no shortage of examples. For the first time, players without contracts in place were welcome in camp. That led to player walkouts and threats. Pete Rose, one of five unsigned Reds, didn't walk, but he also didn't sign his contract until the last day of camp.

When the Texas Rangers made their first Tampa appearance on March 29, they were without their manager, Frank Lucchesi, who was in an Orlando hospital after being punched by infielder Lenny Randle the day before. In a 7–6 win over the Phillies on April 3 at Al Lopez Field, Rose's brother Dave, a Tampa resident, was involved in a fistfight in the stands with a fan who cursed the unsigned Pete as he kneeled in the on-deck circle.

While St. Petersburg was christening a shiny new Al Lang Stadium, the *Tampa Tribune* wrote a story on February 13 detailing how Al Lopez Field was literally falling apart. Among the issues: holes in the grandstand roof, condemned bleachers in left field, foul line fences battered, unstable lockers and considerably more.

Pete Rose leads spring training calisthenics at Redsland. *Courtesy of the Rhodes/Klumpe Reds Hall of Fame Collection.*

And then there was the worst news of all: The Big Red Machine ran out of gas. "As spring wore on, some inner doubts developed," wrote Sparky Anderson in his book *The Main Spark*. "My inside concern in the spring had to do with possible loss of sense of reality by our players. After the ecstasy of two World Championships, it would be dangerous I felt to go into the season too high. I saw it happening early. I should have moved in. We were walking on air much of spring training. We weren't touching ground. My term for hard work is 'grinding.' By God, we weren't grinding."

And the media picked up on it. On April 1, 1977, the *Tampa Tribune* wrote, "Some of the Reds appear to be only going through the motions of playing."

Anderson wrote more about it. "One day in Tampa, sensing that some players were just going through the motions, I whispered, 'Look at 'em. They don't want to play. It's a hot day and they don't want to be out there. I don't blame 'em. I don't want to be out here managing either.'"

He took notice of how many players begged off on taking spring road trips, using the excuse that they could get more work in with a couple of coaches at Al Lopez Field than by playing in games. Anderson told the *Tribune*, "We have been lackadaisical. The water has been running cold all spring."

Left: Al Lopez's Hall of Fame plaque. *Photo by Rick Vaughn.*

Right: Sparky Anderson studying his team at Al Lopez Field. *Courtesy of the Rhodes/Klumpe Reds Hall of Fame Collection.*

As it turned out, the Reds weren't the only ones whose effort was being called into question. On a Sunday afternoon late in March, a season-high crowd of 6,861 watched the Reds beat the Yankees again, 4–3, in ten innings in a rematch of the 1976 World Series.

Rookie Ray Knight's single to right field scored Champ Summers from second base with the winning run. Instead of throwing home, the Yankees' new free agent right fielder, Reggie Jackson, fielded the ball and inexplicably began running with it toward the visiting dressing room while Summers limped home with the winning run after apparently suffering a muscle pull.

The *Tampa Tribune* wrote, "The crowd was puzzled more than anything else, wondering if they were wrong, if they understood the rules, wondering why Jackson made no attempt to get the runner at the plate. The drama of the afternoon seemed to fizzle out, leaving all a little slack and disappointed."

After the game, Yankees manager Billy Martin said he believed Jackson had tendinitis in his throwing arm but offered little else.

"I know this," said Knight afterward, "He [Martin] pitched Don Gullet, Dick Tidrow and Sparky Lyle and they're three pretty good pitchers and the only change he made to his lineup [from the World Series] was at catcher and in the outfield so he must have wanted to win."

In talking to Tom McEwen of the *Tampa Tribune* later back at the team hotel, Jackson only made it worse: "I've never had a sore arm before. It hurts to lift it. I shouldn't have played, but I felt a responsibility. We were playing the Reds and Mr. Steinbrenner lives in Tampa. So, I played the full ten innings. I was surprised I played so long, but there I was. Now, I should know people are waiting on you to make a mistake. But, well, I pulled a bonehead play. I could have lobbed it in. I could have rolled it underhand. I could have done more than I did. The way things turned out they may have gotten the guy [Summers]. But I didn't and I am not going to be the one to cry. I'm not going to be the one to say I had a sore arm and that's why I didn't throw the ball. I say I made a bad play. I should have gone through the motions. But I didn't and I'll eat it. Yet, in the long run, the important thing is the arm, isn't it?"

(As it turned out, the incident was the first sign of what was to come for the Yankees that tumultuous season marred by jealousy, bickering and fighting, yet somehow ending with a World Championship. Less than three

Pete Rose wearing the Reds' St. Patrick's Day uniform in 1978 with Tampa Stadium in the background. *Courtesy of the Rhodes/Klumpe Reds Hall of Fame Collection.*

THE CINCINNATI GREENS

Innovation was long part of the Reds spring training camps in Tampa. There were radio broadcasts of spring training games as early as 1935. Cincinnati was Major League Baseball's first team to visit Puerto Rico, in 1936. The Reds held possibly spring training's first Latin America Day in 1938. They hosted the Grapefruit League's first doubleheader at Plant Field in 1947. Led by Ted Kluszewski, the Reds were among the first to utilize video cameras and film study. Manager Luke Sewell constructed what may have been the first "indoor" pitching mounds, in 1951. The team experimented with yellow bases and foul lines in 1954. The Reds debuted their iconic red vests in 1955 and wore "air-conditioned" caps in 1958. General Manager Gabe Paul hired a target-shooting expert in 1959 to help sharpen the players' vision skills, and in 1961, Manager Fred Hutchinson introduced his "night school."

And on St. Patrick's Day 1978, there was another first, this one a surprise. The Reds were the "Greens," sporting green caps and white uniforms complete with a shamrock on the left sleeve before a season-high 7,043 fans, who saw the Reds stymie the Yankees, 9–2. In doing so, they started a modern-day trend duplicated many times since. "Confused Yankees Can't Find Reds, Bow to Greens, 9–2," was the headline in the *Cincinnati Enquirer*.

The idea sprang from a suggestion made by promotions director Roger Ruhl. Even the players were unaware of the new look until they entered the clubhouse after batting practice. The only misstep? The Reds forgot to order green batting helmets.

What made the day even more special was the fact that the Reds scored all 9 of their runs off a pair of future Hall of Famers in Catfish Hunter and Goose Gossage.

months later, Martin and Jackson went at it on national television in the visiting dugout at Fenway Park after Martin pulled his star in the middle of an inning for not hustling. Their feud would last until Martin was fired in 1978, the first of his four firings ordered by George Steinbrenner.)

Anderson, in the winning locker room, said only that he knew that as hot as Knight had been all spring, the Reds had a good chance to score in the tenth, but the Reds manager had his own problems. He spoke to the team about it before the final game of the spring. "I told them that if I was a man who liked to vomit, I'd vomit," he admitted later to the *Tampa Tribune*'s Jim Selman. "It was the worst camp I ever saw."

Although they won eighty-eight games, the sputtering machine finished ten games back. "It turned out to be bluntly speaking," wrote Anderson, "an awful year."

The Reds wouldn't win another postseason game for thirteen years. "My first camp was in 1980," recalled Tom Foley. "I was there with Rose, Bench, Perez, Concepción and George Foster, guys I grew up watching. But by then we knew it was probably the end of The Big Red Machine. We called ourselves the 'little train who thought we could.'"

Tampanians may have been frustrated by the Reds' on-the-field issues in 1977, but it didn't stop them from coming. For the first time in Tampa spring training history, more than 50,000 paid customers entered the gates, and in nine of the fourteen games it was standing-room-only. In 1978, they broke 50,000 again, and their average of 5,075 was second in all of baseball behind the Fort Lauderdale–based Yankees.

MARCH 14, 1978. George Foster hit 3 solo home runs and a double to lead the Reds past the Cardinals, 11–10.

APRIL 1, 1978. Tom Seaver earned the win and fellow Hall of Famer Bert Blyleven the loss as the Reds thumped the Pirates, 10–2. Dan Driessen singled, tripled, homered and drove in 5 runs. Dave Parker, headed for his second straight NL batting title, homered off Seaver.

MARCH 26, 1979. The Cardinals' George Hendrick hit a 3-run home run and a grand slam in an 11–4 win over the Reds. Hendrick also assisted on his friend George Foster's 3-run homer, which glanced off Hendrick's glove on its way over the center-field fence at Al Lopez Field.

JUST ANOTHER FRIDAY IN TAMPA

On April 3, 1981, the Reds' thirty-six-year-old Tom Seaver pitched seven innings and allowed 3 earned runs in a 5–4 loss to the Mets at Al Lopez Field. Less than four miles away at the same time, Dwight Gooden was also pitching. The sixteen-year-old Tampa native matched Seaver's seven innings for Hillsborough High School and earned an 8–1 win over at rival Leto. Gooden chipped in with 2 hits and 3 RBI.

LaRussa Back in His Sixth Different Uniform

After playing at Al Lopez Field in games with the Colt League, American Legion, Florida State League, Florida Instructional League and Grapefruit League, Tony LaRussa returned in yet another role: manager of the Chicago White Sox, on March 30, 1981, in an 8–3 loss to the Reds. His father, Tony, and Al Lopez were there with him that day in the dugout before the game. "Don't think for a minute this isn't something very special to me to sit in the dugout at Comiskey Park, to sit here and manage where Al Lopez did," LaRussa told the *Tampa Tribune*.

MARCH 11, 1982. Tom Seaver retired the first batter of the game, and then the next eight Pirates hit safely off him as the Reds fell, 13–7. Seaver, who worked two innings and allowed 11 hits and 10 runs, was nursing a left thigh injury. "What happened was not a surprise," he said afterward in Lopez Field's home clubhouse. "The leg isn't 100 percent yet. But the number one thing on my mind wasn't to aggravate it and I don't think I did. My shoulder felt terrific and everything else was fine." Except he wasn't. Plagued by a series of health issues, Seaver made only twenty-one starts that season and suffered through his worst season, posting a 5-13 record and a career-high 5.50 earned run average.

MARCH 14, 1982. Rookie Gary Redus hit a walk-off grand slam in the ninth inning to give the Reds a 3–2 win. Confused? Redus didn't realize the ball had cleared the fence and stopped running between first and second. He was credited with a game-winning RBI single. Another rookie, Vada Pinson, had a similar incident at Al Lopez Field in 1959, also losing a walk-off grand slam.

APRIL 1, 1982. A two-out, pinch-hit single in the top of the eleventh inning by Lou Piniella gave the Yankees a 3–2 win over the Reds. Many in the crowd of 6,440 at Al Lopez Field chanted, "Lou…Lou…Lou…." The night before, the Yankees defeated the University of South Florida, 9–1, at USF's Red McEwen Field.

MARCH 14, 1983. Jim Rice hit a home run, Dennis Eckersley pitched four scoreless innings and Tampa's Wade Boggs had 2 hits to lead Boston to an 8–2 win over the Reds at Al Lopez Field.

THE UMPIRE STRIKES BACK!

During the first week of the Reds' 1983 camp, Cincinnati left-handed pitcher Charlie Leibrandt was in a dogfight to make the team's twenty-five-man roster. According to the *Tampa Tribune*, Leibrandt was running with the other pitchers in the outfield at Redsland when he was bitten by a dog on the upper left leg. The dog was owned by the son of umpire Augie Donatelli, Pat, who was on-site to do some painting for the Tampa Sports Authority. A dog lover, Leibrandt was given a tetanus shot, and the dog, who was up to date on his shots, was kept under observation and returned to Donatelli.

MARCH 23, 1983. Vida Blue worked five innings and walked 8 batters but allowed only 2 runs to earn an 8–2 win over the Reds in his Al Lopez Field debut. In his fifteenth major league season, Blue went 0-5 during the regular season for the Royals.

MARCH 30, 1984. In Kansas City's 5–3 win at Al Lopez Field, George Brett had a single in 3 at bats but suffered a knee injury that kept him out of the season's first seven weeks and limited him to 104 games, his fewest for one season over his twenty-one-year career. Brett partially tore the medial collateral ligament in his left knee while awkwardly trying to field a single to left field by the Reds' Nick Esasky.

JULY 1984. The Florida State League Tampa Tarpons had an unheard-of ten games rained out at Al Lopez Field in July. Poor drainage was blamed.

FEBRUARY 22, 1985. Pete Rose returned to Tampa as player-manager of the Reds. According to the *Tampa Tribune*, the media contingent at Redsland for that first workout was "perhaps the largest in team history. "Well," quipped Rose, "I have more hits than all the managers combined."

MARCH 8, 1986. In his last spring training, forty-three-year-old Tony Perez hit a grand slam and added an RBI single in the spring opener for the Reds, a 7–4 win over the Phillies before 6,294 fans. Perez's slam went over the Al Lopez outfield sign that read, "Sun City Center: Florida's Premier Retirement Home."

APRIL 5, 1986. The Braves scored 6 runs in the ninth, the last 3 on a home run by Rafael Ramirez, to edge the Reds, 6–5, in the spring finale at Al Lopez Field. With Braves games televised into the Tampa Bay market, many Atlanta supporters were among the season-high crowd of 6,756. For fourteen home dates, the Reds drew a Tampa season record of 68,812, and the revenue received by the Tampa Sports Authority was a record $145,000. It was the Reds' penultimate season in the city.

18

"I COULD WALK IT
WITH MY EYES CLOSED"

O ther than the park's namesake, there may be no one with greater memories of Al Lopez Field than Wade Boggs. "It was a very special place to me," said Wade recently. "It was where I learned that I had been drafted and it was where I learned I was going to the major leagues."

On the day of the June 1976 amateur draft, Wade, a senior at Plant High School, and another highly touted prospect from Tampa, pitcher Sammy Spence, were at the offices of the *Tampa Tribune*. Both were expected to go early in the draft, and the local newspaper wanted their reactions to being selected. Spence was taken in the second round by Cleveland, but after a few hours, Wade's named had not been called. "I had to leave to go home and get dressed for the American Legion game I had at Al Lopez Field," Boggs recalled. "I left thinking I was going to go play for Bobby Richardson at the University of South Carolina."

Hours later, Wade was fielding ground balls during pregame infield practice for Post 139 when his girlfriend, Debbie (now wife of forty-seven years), came running down through the stands, shouting that he had been drafted by the Red Sox in the seventh round. "My dad [Win] was there, too, and we got together at the railing by the dugout and he said, 'That might not be so bad. Fenway Park was made for you.'"

Two days later, a Red Sox scout named George Digby was at Wade's home, and a deal was struck. "My dad told me it was time for me to be a man and that this decision was mine to make. I told him the only thing I ever wanted to do was play major league baseball. He said, 'Well it looks like you're going to be a Red Sock.'"

Six years later, after grinding his way through every level of Boston's minor league system and batting above .300 in five of those seasons, Wade was in big league spring training, trying to make the team of Carl Yastrzemski, Jim Rice, Tony Perez and Dwight Evans. "It was one of the final games of spring training and we were playing the Reds at Al Lopez Field," remembered Boggs. "Johnny Bench was playing that day and at some point, I see him and I called him Mr. Bench. And he said to me, 'Call me Johnny and it looks like you're going to make the ballclub.' I said I don't know about that yet and he said, 'Well, let me be the first to congratulate you then.'"

As it turned out, George Digby, the scout who signed Wade, knew about his promotion. "George let the cat out of the bag. It seemed like everyone else knew but me! Debbie, my dad, they all knew."

When the wrecking ball finally swung and connected at Al Lopez Field in May 1989, after numerous delays, it signaled the end of a long, painful death for the thirty-three-year-old cathedral bearing the name of the city's most beloved figure. "Personally, I think he (Lopez) was devastated when the stadium was torn down, but he's not the kind of man that would go out and pop off about it," Lopez's longtime friend Tony Saladino told the *St. Petersburg Times*. "He's the only man in history to outlive a monument built in his honor, and there was nothing in lieu of (the destruction)."

Said Lopez to the *St. Petersburg Times*: "Naturally, at the time the stadium was torn down, I thought they were going to build a bigger and a better one. Unfortunately, that didn't happen. It's kinda sad to tear it down and make a parking lot out of it. There's been some great players who played there." To be exact, ninety-three future Hall of Famers graced Al Lopez Field.

Its actual demise began nearly seven years before, on November 15, 1982, when the Tampa Sports Authority voted to pursue a major league baseball franchise either through expansion or relocation. Further, it was a financial advantage to the city and county to put a new stadium on the Al Lopez Field grounds. The field itself, as Lopez lamented, would indeed become a parking lot.

The TSA announcement was provoked by the Pinellas County Sports Authority, which had launched a similar initiative in February 1980. The headline in the December 7, 1982 edition of the *St. Petersburg Times* blared, "St. Pete and Tampa Begin Game of Hardball." The rivalry that began in 1913 was about to resume.

The wrecking ball claims Al Lopez Field in 1989. *Courtesy of WFLA-TV.*

On April 25, 1984, Tampa Bay auto magnate Frank Morsani and the Tampa Bay Baseball Group (TBBG) went so far as to purchase 42 percent of the Minnesota Twins with the intent on moving the team to Tampa. Less than three months later, at the urging of Commissioner Bowie Kuhn and with assurances from baseball owners that Tampa would be awarded the next expansion team, TBBG sold its share to Carl Pohlad, who had just purchased the majority of the Twins' ownership in June.

The *Tampa Tribune*'s Tom McEwen quoted one baseball insider as saying, "Denver, Tampa, lead pipe cinch" when it came to expansion. It never happened. Morsani also had agreements to buy the Oakland A's and Texas Rangers. Almost predictably, both fell through.

As the two Tampa Bay cities continued to race to see which side could get a stadium built first with visions of their own major league franchise, the uncertainty of the Al Lopez Field site forced the Reds to consider other alternatives. Suitors ranging from Port Charlotte, Port St. Lucie, Plant City, Coconut Creek, Pompano Beach and Palm Bay were under consideration.

When the Reds gathered in Tampa each spring in the 1980s, they were unsure if it would be there last spring there, as the TSA continually repeated that Al Lopez Field would be demolished.

The team held a lease through 1987 and wished it to be extended, but the TSA wanted no part of a long-term arrangement. They were putting all their chips in the middle of the table: A major league franchise of their own or nothing. Either way, the creaky, beloved ballpark was coming down. "Our thought is that if the baseball group does not get a team, we probably won't get another spring training team," said TSA chairman Lon Hatton at the time. Fortunately for Tampanians, he would eventually be proven wrong.

The Reds were left with no choice, and in January 1987, they reached an agreement with Plant City on a $7 million spring training home that would be ready the following spring and be modeled after the Texas Rangers' spring facility in Port Charlotte.

While the Reds' new home would be located just thirty miles east of Tampa off Interstate 4, the fifty-four-year partnership, the longest between a city and a major league club at the time, was over. Excluding the three years that spring training travel was forbidden during World War II, Tampa would be without a major league team for the first March since 1918.

That final spring, there was a gloomy reminder of what was to come. Outside Al Lopez Field's main gate was a billboard declaring it "The Site of Tampa Bay Coliseum" above a sketch of the designed domed stadium to be built there one day. Full-page ads paid for by the Tampa Bay Baseball Group in the *Tribune* carried the same message.

"It's sad," said Jim Hoff, the Reds' player development field coordinator. "I spent half my adult life in that place." Hoff would later hold a similar position with the Tampa Bay Rays.

"I have such great memories there," said veteran infielder Tom Foley, who played his first games in a major league uniform at Al Lopez Field. "It was my first experience in major league baseball, and I thought was a great park, everything about it."

Tino Martinez, who played one of his sixteen seasons in the major leagues with his hometown Devil Rays, remembered getting to play on Al Lopez Field only twice. "We played the semi-final and final games of the 1982 state high school championship there my freshman year at Tampa Catholic, and it was incredible playing on a major league field," recalled Martinez. "There were four thousand to five thousand people in the park. It was packed. It was such a great experience for us. It left such an impression on me."

Dwight Gooden also had nothing but good memories. "Sometimes my dad would just drop us off at the games. He'd give us money to get in, but we would sneak in so we could save it to buy hot dogs and cokes. We had a place in right field that worked every time," he recalled to the *Tampa Tribune*.

Hal McCoy, who covered the Reds as a beat writer for the *Dayton Daily News* for thirty-seven years, recalled how the Reds' writers never went to the ballpark's press box. "The left field bleachers were seldom occupied," McCoy wrote in his book *The Real McCoy*. "We writers used it as our auxiliary press box sitting in the sun with our shirts off." The Reds' bullpen was located directly in front of the writers' makeshift perch. Security in those times was a bit relaxed, so it wasn't long before McCoy moved down the bleachers and sat with the relief pitchers on the bullpen bench. "Once in a while I would grab a glove and warm up the left fielder between innings," he recalled. "One day I picked up a baseball and autographed it. Between innings, George Foster ran to his position in left field and I began tossing the ball back and forth with him. On the fourth toss, he looked at the ball, spotted my signature and lobbed the ball over the left field wall."

Prior to the Reds' final game there, Tony Perez told the *Tribune*: "Here is where I prepared myself for the big leagues. This is where I grew up. I could walk it with my eyes closed."

Ritter Collett, sports editor of the *Dayton Daily News* who began covering the Reds in 1947, told the *Tampa Tribune*: "It is odd. It is very sad. A city like Tampa, a city that has grown so much, I would think would have room for spring training."

Twenty-three-year-old Tony Perez at Al Lopez Field, where he spent sixteen springs. *Courtesy of the Rhodes/Klumpe Reds Hall of Fame Collection.*

142

But for at least two locals, friends who would hold their own batting practice sessions together on the way up major league's ladder, some very special memories were still to be made. On March 12 in that final spring, Mets rookie third baseman Dave Magadan, who attended neighboring Jesuit High School, hit a home run in his first at bat and doubled home the winning run in the ninth inning of the Mets' 6–5 win over the Reds in his Al Lopez Field debut.

While his school was only a couple hundred yards from the field, Magadan had never actually stepped on it. "It's hard to believe, but it's true," he told the *St. Petersburg Times*. "I've never played here. This was fun, though. My family and a lot of my friends got to see me play. That doesn't happen very often."

Three weeks, later, on March 31, his friend, Jefferson High School's Fred McGriff, hit 2 home runs and added a single and 3 runs batted in to lead Toronto to a 15–8 win over the Reds at Al Lopez Field. The blows gave McGriff 7 home runs for the spring, guaranteeing the twenty-three-year-old a roster spot. "To me," said Blue Jays manager Jimy Williams, "he's ready. He can't do much more than what he's done except take tickets."

Later that week, on April 3, Reds rookie Lloyd McClendon hit a lead-off home run in the tenth inning that gave the Reds an 8–7 win over the Astros in what would be the final game at Al Lopez Field. McClendon's blast came off a Lopez—the Astros' Aurelio Lopez. The final game at its predecessor, Plant Field, also ended with a walk-off home run.

The next day, another major league team left Tampa Bay as the Mets played their last game in St. Petersburg, ending a twenty-six-year affiliation. Their next spring training game would be in Port St. Lucie.

Pete Rose, who played in 135 spring training games at Al Lopez Field and managed another 36, told the *Tribune* before the Reds' last game, "It was the first place I ever hit .300," something he did seventeen times during his professional career. "I will miss Tampa. This is a fine place, a beautiful place. I probably will continue to live here in the spring."

It may have been Russ Nixon, who managed the Reds and the Tarpons, who knew the place better than anyone else. "My paycheck [with the Tarpons] was $150 a week and I had a wife and four kids at home," he told the *Tampa Tribune*. "I couldn't afford to have them come down and stay with me so I slept in the clubhouse for three years."

Another former Reds manager, Sparky Anderson, weighed in on the field's demise from Lakeland, where he was piloting the Tigers. "I feel very sad," he told WFLA-TV. "That's where I started my career and where all the good stuff happened."

SCHOOL DAYS DIDN'T ALWAYS INCLUDE SCHOOL

Lou Piniella and Tony LaRussa, who managed against each other in the 1990 World Series, were about a year apart in age and attended different Tampa high schools, but both had the same idea.

Recalled LaRussa years later to the *Tampa Tribune*, "'I can remember how I'd sneak over from my school in West Tampa [Jefferson High School] and sneak in to see Minnie Miñoso play and watch Al Lopez manage the White Sox or see the Reds play....Don Newcombe or Vada Pinson.

"I snuck in 10 or 12 times and finally Manny [beloved police officer Manny DeCastro, whose beat included Al Lopez Field] would stop me and say 'Son, I know your momma and pappa and you are making them very ashamed. Now what's your name?'"

Piniella laughed when asked about his first memories of the ballpark. Lou was another one of the Tampa products who grew up playing baseball during the summers from 8:00 a.m. to 10:00 p.m. His father pitched on Sundays in the Tampa semipro Intersocial League. Lou was often the bat boy.

The three-time manager of the year admitted that while a student at Jesuit High School, he would skip school during spring training to catch Reds games at the park, located a short walk from Jesuit. "I would stand outside and chase down home runs and foul balls during batting practice and sell the balls for a quarter until I had enough money to buy a ticket."

Until one day, when it all went wrong. "I was going through the stands and who did I see but Father Lashley from Jesuit who happened to be taking in the game himself," recounted Piniella. "That ended that."

Boggs agreed. "Growing up that's the only place I ever saw a major league game," he said recently. "If you played Legion ball, you played there. Everyone knew that ballpark. It had gotten pretty rundown but it seemed like such a waste."

The Florida State League's Tampa Tarpons were the last to leave. The team's owners negotiated a deal with the TSA to play one more season at Al Lopez Field, and on August 28, 1988, the last baseball game was played at the beloved, historic diamond. The Tarpons, in their first year as a White Sox affiliate, defeated the Port Saint Lucie Mets, 6–1. A journeyman outfielder named Dan Wagner hit a home run and drove in 4 runs.

Al Lopez was honored at Ybor City's Centro Asturiano while Al Lopez Field was being torn down. *Courtesy of Tampa Baseball Museum.*

Eight months later, it was all gone, victim of Tampa's fruitless effort to land a major league club. Numerous leverage plays by other major league teams naming Tampa Bay as a possible landing site served only to exasperate officials from both sides of the bay.

R.V. Shulnberg, president of Eagle Demolition, which was awarded the contract for the project, regularly attended Reds games there. "It's like going back to the old neighborhood you lived in as a kid and seeing a super highway running through your backyard," he was quoted as saying in the *Tampa Tribune*. "But anytime you tear something down it's because something else is going to be more useful."

There are exceptions to everything.

At the same time that Eagle Demolition was running ads in the classified section of the local papers selling Al Lopez Field bleachers, stadium seats, light towers, scoreboard and wood fencing, city and state leaders were planning Al Lopez Day. The festivities were capped by an elegant dinner at one of El Señor's favorite hangouts, Ybor City's Centro Asturiano, hosted by Richard and Adele Gonzmart of the Columbia Restaurant. The highlight of the evening was Lopez, having never finished high school, receiving an honorary degree from the University of South Florida. If the timing of the event was meant to ease Lopez's pain, it appeared to have worked.

"I've never seen such an outpouring of friendship," Lopez told the audience that night. Among the many stories the humbled eighty-year-old Lopez shared was one recounted later by the *Tribune*'s Tom McEwen. "I'll never forget," began Lopez, "I had just finished my first year in the majors with Brooklyn and came home for the offseason in a new Ford coupe. I parked it just outside here on Nebraska [Avenue], came in here to see my friends and play dominoes. Someone told me to look out the window. I did and two guys were taking two wheels off my car. What's more, they were friends of mine. I yelled at them and told them it was my car. They put the tires back on, said they were sorry and went on."

"Someone in the audience," noted McEwen, "mentioned that in some ways, some things never change."

In 1992, after failing to realize the dream of building a major league stadium on the Al Lopez Field grounds, the city again dedicated the space to Al Lopez. On October 3, 1992, a statue and plaque were dedicated at the new Al Lopez Park. According to the city's website, the park includes 132 acres offering a nature trail, freshwater ponds and a community center. It makes no mention of a baseball diamond.

19

LEGENDS OF THE SPRING

Seventy-one years after they first arrived in the Tampa Bay area and thirty-five years since they left, the New York Yankees were back. It was in June 1924 that Al Lang first enticed the reigning World Champions to come to St. Petersburg by building them a $40,000 practice facility.

To bring George Steinbrenner's twenty-two-time World Champions to Tampa in 1996, it cost a little more. The Tampa Sports Authority built the Yankees' new Legends Field home for $31 million. Tampa had first made a pitch to get the Yankees in 1919, but owner Jacob Ruppert decided on Jacksonville, spurning both Tampa and Al Lang in St. Petersburg.

While the negotiation dance between the Yankees and the TSA took years and was interrupted by overtures from Pasco County, Kissimmee and Orlando, there was never really any doubt that Steinbrenner's team would eventually end up in Tampa. The larger-than-life mogul had moved his family and his shipbuilding business to Tampa in 1976. Evidence of his community work could be found far and wide. Plus, for years, the Yankees organization had conducted business meetings at his Bay Harbor Inn Hotel, located near the Bay area's Courtney Campbell Causeway.

When the Reds left Tampa for Plant City, Steinbrenner saw his chance, with a particular interest in Redsland, the twenty-one-year-old training complex. Steinbrenner was looking to improve the Yankees' own minor league facility in Fort Lauderdale. While negotiations continued with that city's officials, the Yankees' owner sent a proposal to the TSA in September 1988 to move their minor league operations to Tampa for two years.

George Steinbrenner at one of the many charitable events he hosted in the Tampa Bay area. *Courtesy of Library of Congress.*

The TSA took little time in accepting, hoping that the mere presence of the Yankees' minor league camp might enhance their profile with Major League Baseball's owners. In 1989, the Yankees would bring approximately two hundred players and staff from their six minor league affiliates for what would be their spring camp, winter instructional league and an injury rehabilitation center during the summer. Steinbrenner insisted the team's minor leaguers would not stay at the Bay Harbor Inn as a gesture of increasing revenue opportunities for local businesses.

In addition to a new name, Redsland was badly in need of renovation. The Yankees and TSA shared the costs on the field upgrades, and the team renovated what had been the Reds' somewhat austere offices.

A few months after their first minor league camp ended, the Yankees signed a two-year extension, and in 1992, the "Core Four"—Derek Jeter, Andy Pettitte, Mariano Rivera and Jorge Posada—along with Bernie Williams, gathered for the first time in mid-September at the organization's instructional league camp. Bill Livesey, the Yankees' vice-president of scouting and development, remembered it well. "That summer, Peter Gammons had written a piece in the *Boston Globe* about our minor league system that was not very flattering, that we lacked prospects," Livesey recalled. "George [Steinbrenner] would not allow us to provide information, any information on our players, so Peter didn't have much to go on."

Still stinging a bit from the *Globe* story, Livesey told Yankees farm director Mitch Lukevics, "We're going to bring every single prospect we have to the instructional league." That camp's roster not only included the Core Four but also other key prospects, some of whom would be traded to bring the likes of David Cone, Tino Martinez and Paul O'Neill into the fold. It all led to an eighteen-year span in which the Yankees advanced to the postseason seventeen times.

"Peter came down to Tampa and did a show for ESPN from our camp that fall and it was a little different tone than the article," Livesey added, chuckling. "I think we had something like 60 future major leaguers in instructional league over a five-year span."

With the construction of St. Petersburg's Florida Suncoast Dome underway, Tampa's discussions regarding relocation of the Yankees' major league spring camp escalated. Still, it took another four years to reach the finish line while the TSA was balancing a variety of different venue location options for the city's new National Hockey League team, the Lightning, and the Buccaneers. In October 1993, the Hillsborough County Commissioners opened the door for the Yankees by voting five to two in favor of building a ten-thousand-seat stadium to be located across the street from the former Al Lopez Field site. A ground-breaking event was held on October 21, 1994, just four months and sixteen days before St. Petersburg would be awarded the area's expansion franchise. Opening Day at the Yankees' new home would be March 1, 1996. Tampa would become the team's twenty-fourth different spring training home, and the Yankees would be the seventh Grapefruit League team to call Tampa home.

The excitement surrounding the Yankees and their new ballpark quickly became evident when six games sold out before the major leaguers even reported to camp that first spring. It was not at all unexpected. The Yankees drew the Al Lopez Field season-high in eighteen of the twenty springs they visited the park, including 8,350 on March 17, 1963, the largest paid crowd in Tampa's Grapefruit League history. Of Lopez Field's ten largest crowds of all time, eight were games with the Yankees.

Outside Legends Field, near a garden of beautiful flowers, were plaques honoring Ruth, Gehrig, Mantle, Maris, DiMaggio, Berra, Rizzuto, Ford and

Legends Field in its first year, 1996. *Tampa Bay Times photo.*

Stengel. "It's the best [complex] I've been to," said New York's first-year manager, Joe Torre. "It's beautiful."

Opening Day brought gray skies and cool, damp weather, but there were 9,928 people in the stands when the Yankees beat the Indians, 5–2. Grammy-winning trumpeter Al Hirt performed the National Anthem, Yankees Hall of Famer Phil Rizzuto threw out the first pitch, Yankee Stadium voice Bob Shepherd supplied the public address and coach Don Zimmer became the first to wear a uniform at Plant Field, Al Lopez Field and Legends. Major League Baseball was back in Tampa after an eight-year absence.

Albert Belle hit a 2-run homer off David Cone in the first inning. Wade Boggs's RBI single in the third inning gave the Yankees their first run. "I've been involved in Opening Days during the major league season that weren't like Opening Day here," Torre told the *St. Petersburg Times.* "It was a big day. I'm just glad we christened it with a win."

Steinbrenner was beaming. "Is there anything better than this?" he exclaimed to his friends surrounding him in his box. "We wanted this to be a centerpiece of sports in Tampa, something the whole area could be proud of. We wanted to make everything first class."

He left nothing to chance. The *New York Times* observed, "The Yankees' owner directed traffic in the parking lot and Joseph Malloy, Steinbrenner's son-in-law, used towels to dry dozens of seats before fans entered the sparkling facility."

Vince Naimoli, owner of the expansion Devil Rays, which would begin play in St. Petersburg in 1998, said, "Everybody I know agrees it is the new standard for spring facilities."

Rick Nafe, the humorous executive director of the TSA and one of the architects of the stadium deal, joked, "George wanted the facility to have the same feel as Yankee Stadium, so we're putting a few burned-out automobiles in the parking lot, and will arrange to have you mugged every three weeks."

In the second week of camp, Steinbrenner held the first of his famous impromptu media sessions, standing on the grass at the new park. This one lasted forty-five minutes. "We can't take three years and rebuild. We are the New York Yankees," he lectured the media throng. "We're the number one road draw in all of baseball. I can't lay back and bring younger kids in. We have a burden that not a lot of teams carry."

But there was one "younger kid" in that first camp that Torre and many others were keeping their eyes on. The early drama of the spring was over the battle for the starting shortstop position. The competition between thirty-three-year-old veteran and four-time Gold Glove winner Tony Fernandez and Derek Jeter, four months shy of his twenty-third birthday, lasted until Fernandez fractured his right elbow diving for an infield single at Legends in an 8–3 win over the Astros on March 24. For the next seventeen seasons, there would be no competition at shortstop for the Yankees, ending a drought that had seen them employ twenty-three players at that position over the previous ten seasons.

On the same day, a highlight of the spring occurred when eighty-one-year-old Joe DiMaggio threw out the ceremonial first pitch to Yankees catcher Jim Leyritz. In the spring finale on March 30, the Mets beat the Yankees, 5–3. The crowd of 10,279 brought the total for the season to 173,234, an average of 10,190 per game.

The Yankees' first spring in Tampa sent them on their way to a World Series title, their first of four in a five-year span. On his arrival back home after the ticker-tape parade along Broadway's "Canyon of Heroes," Steinbrenner received a plaque from the Tampa City Council congratulating him on the World Championship and for his "resolute commitment to Tampa."

The glow of the 1996 World Series Championship season made Legends Field's second Opening Day almost as impressive as its first. Joe Torre's brother, Frank, recent recipient of a heart transplant, threw out the first pitch, the World Championship flag was raised and Tampa native Tony LaRussa was in the visiting dugout as the second-year manager of the Cardinals. His eighty-five-year-old father, Tony Sr., was in the stands. Another Tampa native, Dwight Gooden, pitched the first three innings of the Yankees' 7–3 win before 10,227 fans.

The ballpark was renamed Steinbrenner Field on March 27, 2008, when the "Boss" was in failing health. He died at Tampa's St. Joseph's Hospital in 2010. A life-size bronze statue of the late owner was placed in front of the ballpark the following January. In April 2016, the Yankees and the Tampa Sports Authority came to terms on a $40 million renovation of Steinbrenner Field that extended the team's lease through 2046. New loge boxes, shaded cabanas and a two-story gift shop were added.

Steinbrenner Field, formerly Legends Field, in 2023. *Courtesy of Savannah Bananas.*

Two weeks before he was elected the forty-fourth president of the United States on November 4, 2008, Senator Barack Obama spoke to a crowd of approximately ten thousand at a rally at Steinbrenner Field. Obama was introduced by six players from the recently crowned American League Champion Tampa Bay Rays.

In their first twenty-five spring seasons at Legends/Steinbrenner Field that were not interrupted by COVID-19 or the MLB player lockout, the Yankees averaged more than ten thousand in twenty of them. And, with their Florida State League team back under a Yankees flag beginning in 1994, Tampa was, in fact, at the center of Florida spring training baseball.

WORKS CITED

Books

Burick, Si, and Spark Anderson. *The Main Spark: Sparky Anderson and the Cincinnati Reds*. New York: Doubleday Publishing, 1978.

Cannon, Jason. *Charlie Murphy: The Iconoclastic Showman Behind the Chicago Cubs*. Lincoln: University of Nebraska Press, 2002.

Flood, Curt, and Richard Carter. *The Way It Is*. New York: Trident Press, 1971.

Griffey, Ken, Sr., and Phil Pepe. *Big Red: Baseball, Fatherhood and My Life in the Big Red Machine*. Chicago: Triumph Books, 2014.

McCoy, Hal. *The Real McCoy: My Half Century with the Cincinnati Reds*. Wilmington, OH: Orange Frazer Press, 2015.

Mormino, Gary, and George Pozzetta. *The Immigrant World of Ybor City and Their Latin Neighbors in Tampa, 1885–1985*. Gainesville: University of Florida Press, 2018.

O'Neal, Buck, and David Conrads. *I Was Right on Time: My Journey from Negro Leagues to the Major Leagues*. New York: Simon and Shuster, 1997.

Singletary, Wes. *Al Lopez: The Life of Baseball's El Señor*. Jefferson, NC: McFarland Publishing, 1999.

Weiss, Stuart. *The Curt Flood Story: The Man Behind the Myth*. Columbia: University of Missouri, 2007.

Werber, Bill, and C. Paul Rogers. *Memories of a Ballplayer*. Phoenix, AZ: Society of American Baseball Research, 2001.

Will, George. *Men at Work: The Craft of Baseball*. New York and London: Macmillan Publishers, 1991.

Articles

Covington, James. "The Chicago Cubs Come to Tampa." *Tampa Bay History* 8, no. 1 (1986).
Dunder, Paul. "Baseball, with a Southern Accent: The Urban Game in the Post Reconstruction South." PhD Diss., University of South Florida, 2021.
Jacobsen, Lenny. "Charles Murphy." Society for American Baseball Research. 2011. www.sabr.org.
Savona, David. "From Cigars to the Big Leagues." *Cigar Aficionado* (July–August 2003).

Documentaries

Emett, Mike. Henry B. Plant Museum/Tampa Bay Hotel. Clio: Your Guide to History. August 31, 2016.
HBO, Roy, George and Steven Stern. *Babe Ruth*. 1998.
Video Art and Sunburst Productions. *Baseball From the Beginning*. 2018.
WEDU PBS. *Rise of the Rays: A Devil of a Story*. 2023.

News Outlets

Associated Press
Boston Globe
Chicago American
Chicago Tribune
Cincinnati Enquirer
Cincinnati Post
Dayton (OH) Journal News
Detroit News
Michigan Chronicle (Detroit, MI)
National Baseball Hall of Fame
New York Evening Journal
New York Times

The Sporting News
Sports Illustrated
South Bend (IN) Tribune
St. Petersburg (FL) Times
Tampa (FL) Tribune
United Press International
Washington Evening Star (Washington, D.C.)
WFLA-TV

Special thanks to the National Baseball Hall of Fame, Hillsborough County Library, Pinellas County Library, Sylvia Lind and the Tampa Baseball Museum.

ABOUT THE AUTHOR

Rick Vaughn served for more than thirty years in the sports communications field with MLB's Baltimore Orioles and Tampa Bay Rays and the NFL's Washington Redskins. Afterward, Rick was the director of the Respect 90 Foundation, the charitable organization created by baseball's three-time Manager of the Year Joe Maddon. A 1979 graduate of George Mason University, Rick became a first-time author in 2022 with *100 Years of Baseball on St. Petersburg's Waterfront: How the Game Shaped a City* (Arcadia Press), named as one of the best baseball books of 2022 by *Sports Collector's Digest*. Rick and his wife, Sue, have two daughters, two grandsons and three rescue pups.

Visit us at
www.historypress.com